Curtis'
WESTERN
INDIANS

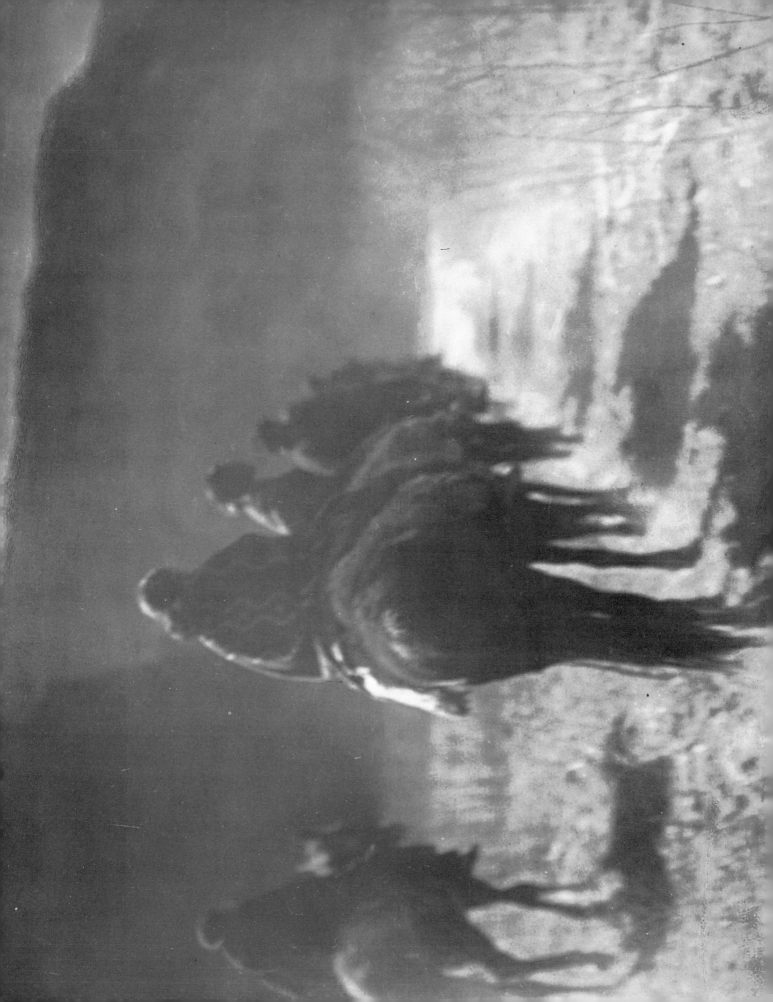

Curtis' WESTERN INDIANS

by

RALPH W. ANDREWS

The Vanishing Race

Symbolic of Indians as a race, already
shorn of tribal strength, stripped of
primitive dress, passing into the darkness of an unknown future, these
Navahos riding into Canyon de Chelly
set the theme that inspired all of Edward Curtis' work.

BONANZA BOOKS · NEW YORK

Library of Congress Card Number 62-14491

This edition published by Bonanza Books,
a division of Crown Publishers, Inc.,
by arrangement with Superior Publishing Company.

b c d e f g h

PRINTED IN THE UNITED STATES OF AMERICA

FOREWORD

IN collecting material for *Indian Primitive* I was impressed with one obvious fact—no one had taken photographs of Indians as had Edward Curtis. As I dug deeper and learned more about this man's work I saw why. He not only had patience and technical skill but he was the Indian's friend, and in the faces of Nootka, Comanche and Apsaroke one could read the character Curtis wanted there.

This admiration for the man's work put me on the way to this book and a v e r y pleasant task it has been to study the personal and public life of the bluff and hearty artist of such virile and courageous proportions, and to inspect his entire published work of over a thousand prints rendered in sepia photogravure. I never knew Edward S. Curtis but after my studies I felt I knew him very well indeed and have formed an intense admiration for his genius.

My own opinions are those of the layman with a limited knowledge of art values and Indian culture. Yet they are well supported by the views of a host of professional evaluators, which includes art critics, editors, ethnologists and curators of I n d i a n artifacts who expressed their appreciation when the first volumes of Curtis' *North American Indian* were published. Wrote Charles M. Kurtz, Director of the Buffalo F i n e Arts Academy:

"There have been a few painters of Indians—but only a few—in comparison with the whole number of artists. In the early days there were George Catlin, Seth Eastman, Charles Wimer, George C. Bingham and Charles B. King. George Catlin alone made a serious study of Indian life. . . .

"It remained for an artist working with the camera to come to the front and avail himself of the opportunity offered by the American Indian—almost at the last moment, but still in time—and to make a series of photographs covering almost every existing tribe, portraying hundreds of various types of character and illustrating methods of life, tribal customs, religious observances, hunting scenes, war dances, etc. In fact, Mr. Edward S. Curtis, who was first attracted to the study of Indian life some ten years ago, has since that time become acquainted with practically every Indian tribe in the United States, has gained the confidence of the Indians, and has established relations with their chiefs, priests and other functionaries, with the result of securing exceptional opportunities for making comprehensive photographic representation of contemporary Indian life. . . .

"Many of these photographs have the qualities one finds in paintings, qualities obtainable only by the artist educated in composition, in the management of light and shadow masses, and the subordination of undue detail when the spirit of the work demands—combined with the skill of the competent photographer knowing all that one should know about necessary periods of exposure under different light effects, the secrets of the development of negatives to produce results most desirable, and a knowledge of making prints that are in the highest degree artistic."

The Portland *Oregonian* stated unequivocally: "Within the past few months, E. S. Curtis, the Seattle artist, has taken by storm art critics, ethnologists, and connoisseurs in their strongest citadels of the East. His marvelous portraits of Indians showing every species of tribal type, illustrating this vanishing race in all its ancient glory, is not only a new revelation in art which appeals to all lovers of the picturesque and beautiful, but as a study of Indian customs and character in all its most subtle and fascinating phases, is an educational work of unique and remarkable value which should be enjoyed by all public school pupils, teachers, students of American history, and the public generally.

"The historical value of this collection has been recognized by the Smithsonian Institution, United States Government, scientists of Washington, D.C. and President Roosevelt, as a matter of international importance. As to the average man and woman, more or less ignorant of Indian life and tradition, the pictures are fascinating in the extreme. . . .

"The touch of the artist is everywhere visible, whether in the marvelous atmospheric effect or the picturesque grouping of the figures. Immense labor has been expended to secure these results. One picture alone, 'The Three Chiefs,' required three visits to Montana and consumed in all three years' time before Mr. Curtis was satisfied with the result."

The Washington (D. C.) *Star,* reviewed the work with great understanding and perception, placing him high in the niche with other portrayers of Indian art. "As Mr. Leupp, the commissioner of Indian affairs, expresses it, Mr. Curtis will enable future generations to see the Indian, not as he has been pictured in romance, or preserved in the mummy wrappings of archaeology, but as he is, in his life, in his mind, in his spirit, in his artistic ideals and sympathies, and in those traditions which afford his people their only substitute for a literature.

"In the '50s a similar work was undertaken in a comparatively small way by Henry R. Schoolcraft of Mackinac Island, Michigan. He published six large volumes which are now very scarce and valuable and worth several times the original price, illustrated by steel engravings from drawings by Capt. Seth Eastman of the army. Congress made an annual appropriation of $5,000 to assist the author to carry on the work, and it was published by the predecessors of the Lippincotts of Philadelphia.

"In 1830 Lord Kingsborough, an English nobleman, began a similar work concerning the aboriginal tribes of the southwest, for the purpose of demonstrating that they were descended from the lost tribes of Israel. It was a monumental undertaking in literature and ethnology and was continued to 1848, when he became bankrupt, having invested his entire fortune. He published nine massive volumes, with many beautiful engravings. The book is very rare and expensive, as the edition was small.

"In 1832, George Catlin, a lawyer and amateur painter of Wilkes Barre, Pennsylvania, went out among the western Indians to obtain portraits, and became so much interested that he abandoned a lucrative practice and devoted the remainder of his life to the patriotic task of preserving the best types of the several tribes. He did nothing else for twenty-five years and produced thousands of Indian portraits in both North and South America. It is a very valuable and interesting collection, both from a historical as well as ethnological standpoint, as it contains the portraits of several famous chieftains.

"The Curtis collection, however, is infinitely more important than those I have referred to because it is not only much more complete and extensive, but has been m a d e upon a thorough system and contains actual photographs of scenes in everyday Indian life that have never been obtained before. They are of much greater value to the ethnologist than mere portraits. They are all accompanied by explanatory notes that add still more to their importance."

And among the hundreds of reviews lauding the Edward S. C u r t i s achievement were the stirring words of Julian Hawthorne. After acknowledging the genius shown in the collection, he made this observation:

"Two things Curtis excluded from his scheme,—speculations as to the origins of the Indians and—so far as possible—the gloomy reiteration of the wrongs done them by the white man. Of both of these the existing literature is already endless, a n d of small profit; and he chose to spend his strength upon filling the gap in the record of their actual lives, occupations, ideas and religions. In this he has done what a hundred men less fortunately endowed and unswervingly devoted might have failed to do; after fifteen years, and in the prime of his manhood, he is already halfway to his goal; and the facility of production increases with each forward step.

"It would be useless to rehearse the contents o f each volume; tribe after tribe i s taken up in turn; representative vocabularies of their many languages are appended; and there are long transcriptions of the discourses of their wise men on t h e i r legends and religious faiths, and on numberless minutiae of rites and usages hitherto unknown or misunderstood. The singularities of Indian hypnotism and catalepsy are portrayed in full; the vigils of their youths, like those of medieval knights; the spiritualization of all natural things and phenomena; the almost universal belief that the earth is the mother of the Indian, and to forsake the portion of her bosom alloted to them at birth, or to tear it open for crops and agriculture, is a fatal sin. Over all dominates the Great Mystery, to which all other deities and powers are subordinate, a n d whose infinite life enters into and actuates all. Hardly an act of an Indian's life but is associated with some religious principle or motive; and the augurs of old Rome were not more solicitous of omens t h a n are these modern sons of an unsearchable past."

For the data and basic information from which I prepared this book I am indebted to several living persons. Miss Harriet Leitch, retired reference librarian of Seattle Public Library, had corresponded at length with Mr. Curtis in his later days and these papers had been given to the library for use as source material. These were handed to me and Miss Leitch voluntarily worked out more than fifty references to newspaper items on the Curtis subject in the Seattle newspapers and national magazines. These were of inestimable help as was the ready cooperation of Seattle Public Library's history section staff in making readily available to me the twenty volumes of the *North American Indian* and corresponding folios of the Curtis prints from which the printing plates of this book were made.

All matters pertaining to the photo-historian's personal and family life, together with many of his manuscripts, notes, magazine articles and photographs were supplied me through interviews with three members of the Curtis family—his sister Eva and daughters Florence and Beth, Mrs. Henry Graybill a n d Mrs. M. E. Magnuson, respectively. Their contributions of anecdotes and intimate touches were invaluable in making the man Edward S. Curtis emerge from the boxes of old records and clippings.

RALPH W. ANDREWS

THE VANISHING RACE

Into the shadow whose illumined crest
    Speaks of the world behind them where the sun
    Still shines for us whose day is not yet done,
Those last dark ones go drifting. East or West,
Or North or South—it matters not, their quest
    Is toward the shadow whence it was begun;
    Hope in it, ah, my brother! there is none;
    And yet—they only seek a place to rest.

So mutely, uncomplainingly they go!
    How shall it be with us when they are gone,
    When they are but a mem'ry and a name?
May not those mournful eyes to phantoms grow—
    When, wronged and lonely, they have drifted on
    Into the voiceless shadow whence they came?

ELLA HIGGINSON

CONTENTS

Photographs Selected from *North American Indian*

Edward S. Curtis

CHAPTER ONE

Sound of Trumpets

The ballroom, converted into an exhibition hall, was lined with pictures almost as large as newspaper pages and mounted on larger boards. Others were hung on both sides of portable display stands arranged so the crowds could move easily around them. The art studies were in brown photogravure to bring out the soft diffusion of detail.

"Who is this Edward S. Curtis?"

The question would be asked a thousand times during the exhibition and again in similar exhibitions in other cities. Who, indeed, was Edward S. Curtis? The program noted him as artist-traveler-historian, that he had spent many years among the Indians, had learned their ways and history as had few Americans. He was engaged in a notable work, a photo-history of all the Western tribes which he considered "The Vanishing Race."

"The pictures are marvelous. I want to hear this lecture. I want to know about this fellow Curtis."

So did the world of culture and everyone who had an interest in the Indians of the United States—and this was almost everyone. For Edward S. Curtis had set about, in 1900, to amass a photo-history of the North American Indian and by the time he had completed it he had made over two thousand published photographs of eighty Western tribes and written the text from his collected notes.

The American Indian was a topic of concern and general interest in 1900. Although he baffled the white man, he incited his curiosity. From the time of Captain John Smith on, the Indian was the subject of endless speculation and comment. Many treatises were published about him. Ethnologists investigated him. Trapper and scout told anecdotes about him. Painters portrayed him. Novelists romanticized and libelled him. Sentimentalists called him "The Noble Savage," the epigrammists said, "The only good Indian is a dead one." One person called him dirty, another treacherous. And in front of all the commotion, the Indian sat wrapped in his blanket, a bronze enigma.

The white man had conquered the Indian and subjected him to his own conditions. Being absorbed into the master race, the "redman" had left his influence upon his captors. Pioneers imitated his way of life, wore his deerskins and moccasins, hunted and fought as he did. They took his women for wives and were not ashamed of the darker blood in their children's veins. Boys played "Indian" in pastures and b a c k yards. Indian words like tomahawk, warpath, paleface and Happy Hunting Grounds crept into the language. The profile of the brave appeared on coins and busts of chiefs appeared as sculpture. And having made this free use of the Indian's life, t h e white man had told him to take the white ways and live with them. The Indian wrapped his blanket tighter and walked away into the shadows, leaving the feeling that all white ways were despicable.

Into this state of confused thought Edward S. Curtis thrust the steadying eye of the camera. He was convinced the Indian had gained nothing from the white man but disease and vice, but being no rabble-rouser, he kept counsel within the circle of his intimates. He had no message of impassioned sentiment nor did he wish to add more dry-as-dust theories to the scientific record. But he was convinced the Indian as a race was quickly disappearing and here was something he could do—make complete and truthful camera impressions, supported by word facts, before the last crest of eagle feathers disappeared into the dark arroyo.

And that is what Edward S. Curtis set out to accomplish. At the time of his decision he was thirty-two years old, a career photographer with hundreds of fine Indian pictures to his credit. His sister Eva recalled later the almost crusading spirit of her older brother in these days.

"He had always been serious minded and busy at something. After our father died, Edward had the full responsibility of the family and he felt the load. There was never any frivolity about him. He would have made a good reporter if he had gone into newspaper work, but as it was he had his camera and a mind so very curious—always nosing into something interesting.

"And how he could concentrate! One of us would ask what he was doing or thinking about or where he had been when he was away from home all day taking pictures of Indians. Most often he didn't seem to hear the question, so preoccupied he was. Taking pictures—that was what he wanted to do above all, pictures of Indians. And now that he was going to spend so much time at it, to make a photographic history of the Indians—well, he seemed all lit up with some fervor of ambition. And then we hardly saw much of him."

Edward Curtis was a strong man, both in convictions and physical vigor. He took on a Herculean task and while he wavered many times in the fulfillment of it, he had the courage and endurance to keep on. He had patience, tact and certain genius in his artistic conception of Indian life and his technical operation of the glass plate camera. He had imagination and intuition. At thirty, he had learned the ancient truth that the way to the center of things is through the heart and sympathies. Enamored from boyhood of the Indian mystery, he gradually built up the great plan of gathering and preserving everything of the Indians—their natures, customs, beliefs and annals— that systematic s t u d y, constant association a n d tireless perseverance could obtain. Aware that another generation would be too late to accomplish this task, he lost himself in it. This was never a pastime or avocation or even a profession. It was his life.

Edward Curtis went to the Indians, not as a critic or patron, not seeking entertainment or attempting to gratify some curiosity. He went as a man to brother man, for the sake of mankind. He went warmly and kindly, with straight looks and honest purpose, without fear or guile. He never admitted the Indians to be an alien people. He sat in their tipis and beside their fires, not as a suppliant or a master, but as a humble equal. He made no secret of his purpose, often content to control his questions u n t i l the right time came to present them.

Yes, he told them, they were doomed to perish from the earth—their old men, women and children—and he would record their story in imperishable f o r m, their lan-

"Homeward Bound"—Curtis' Prize-Winning Photograph

guage, legends, songs, music and above all their impenetrable faces, so that all these would live through the ages. The bronzed men, made suspicious by glib talk from other white men, listened warily and responded ambiguously or not at all. Yet by degree the calm and confident appeal of the lonely student and companion won them over. The boys and girls played their games, the medicine men performed their vows and esoteric rites, the young warriors underwent their torture tests and ceremonial dances, the old women pounded corn and all of them eventually opened the gates of memory and the secret chambers of belief.

They did even more than this. Before the strange and inanimate focus of the camera, they allowed the dances, games, array of battle, smoking of the peace pipe, all that was intimate, occult or active in their lives, to be recorded on plates so other people in future times might know what a great people they were.

The first two volumes of Curtis' *North American Indian* were published i n December, 1907, the result of some seven years of intensive field study. The work had been done by Curtis and his assistants without outside financial aid up to the early months of 1906 when the Morgan Foundation agreed to advance $15,000 a year for five years, and to publish the books as material was made available, twenty volumes in all, the edition limited to five hundred sets. The price per set was to be $3,000.

The New York *Herald* greeted the publication of the first volumes with a three-page review, terming the undertaking "the most gigantic in the making of books since the King James edition of the Bible . . . one that can never be repeated. The author of this stupendous work is Mr. Edward S. Curtis who, as an 'Indianologist' and artistic photo-historian of a vanishing race, is unique in ethnology.

"This gigantic work is being pursued under the patronage and support of Mr. J. Pierpont Morgan and the President of the United States. Mr. Curtis is giving the result of a lifetime of study and work to it. The publication will bring a return of a million and a half dollars, yet this immense sum seems hardly sufficient to cover the expenses of collecting the material and the making of the books. The photogravures and illustrations alone will cost $600,000, the field work adds another item of $250,000 to expense."

As examples of bookmaking, the volumes displayed, as the newspaper stated, "the highest degree of excellence." Bound with the twenty volumes of text were to be fifteen hundred full-page photogravure illustrations, each volume to consist of 350 or more quarto pages, measuring 9½ by 12½ inches.

The printing stock was imported handmade paper of the highest grade, one part of the edition using Holland paper of a rich tone, the other Japan vellum, both selected for their qualities of permanence. The binding was three-quarter Levant, gold top. To accompany each set of text and illustration books were twenty portfolios, each consisting of thirty-six or more copperplate photogravures measuring 12 x 16 inches on 18 x 22 inch sheets. The printing of the books was by University Press of Cambridge, Mass., the photogravures in books and folios, by John Andrew and Son of Boston.

The entire work was edited by Frederick Webb Hodge of the Bureau of American Ethnology and an appreciative foreword to the first volume given by President Theodore Roosevelt. The title page included the statement that the field research was conducted under the patronage of the Morgan Foundation. President Roosevelt wrote:

In Mr. Curtis we have both an artist and a trained observer, whose pictures are pictures, not merely photographs; whose work has far more than mere accuracy, because it is truthful. All serious students are to be congratulated because he is putting his work in permanent form; for our generation offers the last chance for doing what Mr. Curtis has done. The Indian as he has hitherto been is on the point of passing away. His life has been lived under conditions through which our own race passed so many ages ago that not a vestige of their memory remains. It would be a veritable calamity if a vivid and truthful record of these conditions were not kept. No one man alone could preserve such a record in complete form. Others have worked in the past, and are working in the present, to preserve parts of the record; but Mr. Curtis, because of the singular combination of qualities with which he has been blest, and because of his extraordinary success in making and using his opportunities, has been able to do what no other man has ever done; what, as far as we can see, no other man could do. He is an artist who works out of doors and not in the closet. He is a close observer, whose qualities of mind and body fit him to make his observations out in the field, surrounded by the wild life he commemorates. He has lived on intimate terms with many different tribes of the mountains and the plains. He knows them as they hunt, as they travel, as they go about their various avocations on the march and in the camp. He knows their medicine men and their sorcerers, their chiefs and warriors, their young men and maidens. He has not only seen their vigorous outward existence, but has caught glimpses, such as few white men ever catch, into that strange spiritual and mental life of theirs; from whose innermost recesses all white men are forever barred. Mr. Curtis in publishing this book is rendering a real and great service; a service not only to our own people, but to the world of scholarship everywhere.

October 1st, 1906   THEODORE ROOSEVELT

Edward Curtis in Trail Dress

The twenty volumes covered all Indians of the United States, British Columbia and Alaska who still retained to a considerable degree their primitive customs and beliefs. The contents:

Vol. I Apache, Jicarilla Apache, Navaho. *Vol. II* Pima, Papago, Qahitaka, Mohave, Yuma, Maricopa, Walapai, Havasupai, Apache-Mohave. *Vol. III* Teton Sioux, Yanktonai, Assiniboin. *Vol. IV* Apsaroke, Hidatsa. *Vol. V* Mandan, Arikara, Atsina. *Vol. VI* Piegan, Cheyenne, Arapaho. *Vol. VII* Yakima, Klickitat, Interior Salish, Kutenai. *Vol. VIII* Nez Perce, Walla Walla, Umatilla, Cayuse, Chinookan tribes. *Vol. IX* Salishan tribes of the Coast, Chimakum, Quilliute, Willipa. *Vol. X* Kawakiutl.
Vol. XI Nootka, Haida. *Vol. XII* Hopi. *Vol. XIII* Hupa, Yurok, Karok, Wiyot, Tolowa, Tututni, Shasta, Achomawi, Klamath. *Vol. XIV* Kato, Wailaki, Yuki, Pomo, Wintun, Maidu, Miwok, Yokuts. *Vol. XV* Southern California Shoshoneans, Dieguenos, Plateau Shoshoneans, Washo. *Vol. XVI* Tiwa, Keres. *Vol. XVII* Tewa, Zuni. *Vol. XVIII* Chipewyan, Cree, Sarsi. *Vol. XIX* Wichita, Southern Cheyenne, Oto, Comanche. *Vol. XX* Nunivak, King Island, Little Diomede Island, Cape Prince of Wales, Kotzebue.

The first numbered copies of the limited edition were subscribed for almost immediately by the wealthy and public spirited, for their own private collections and for presentation to museums and archives. The list of subscribers included such names as Andrew Carnegie, James J. Hill, Thomas F. Ryan, H. E. Huntington, S. R. Guggenheim, Alexander Graham Bell, Mrs. E. H. Harriman, Mrs. Frederick W. Vanderbilt, Mrs. Herbert Wadsworth, H. M. the King of England and H. M. King Albert, of Belgium. Among the institutions receiving the books were the National Museum of Art, American Museum of Natural History, British Museum, Peabody Museum of Harvard, many college and public libraries throughout the United States and Europe.

A long line of critics, curators, archivists and scientists praised the work at the highest levels. They spoke of feeling great satisfaction that such a skilled photographer was able to expend such an effort and go beyond the limits of most scientific investigators. They touched on the point that this was art as well, true-to-fact art rather than the imaginative brush strokes of painter explorers. And both of these qualities, said the critics and reviewers, would enable future generations to see the Indian, not as he was pictured in romantic stories or preserved in mummy wrappings, but as he lived in body, mind and soul.

Edward Curtis in Field Camp

CHAPTER TWO

Color of a New Land

The tide was in now, the wash from a passing steamboat curling around the tule stems and the bulky legs of the squat Indian woman. There was a harvest sheaf of the plants in the bend of her right arm which grew larger as the left dipped into the water and deftly twisted off more stems. The man standing in the mud of the flat wished the sky would brighten. The fog had already lifted when he brought the Tulalip woman and his camera to the tule bed and for two hours now he had been waiting for the sun to break through with enough light to give some contrasts to the picture. He stood patiently, sniffing the clear air freed from the p u n g e n t low-t i d e smell of the early morning.

Off to the south of the flat a second woman talked in her native tongue, a gutteral Salish. Edward Curtis understood some of her complaint and answered it with short-clipped Indian words. Yes. Walk to there—woman cleaning fish. He pointed to Meta in the tules. Soon. Go clean fish. Picture there soon. "All r i g h t, Meta," he called, bending over in the attitude he wanted her to take. "Good. Stay like that." He sloshed back through the mud to the tripod and thrust his bare head under the black cloth. Then he squeezed the bulb.

Stanley was in Africa, Sidney Norcutt was playing in *The Galley Slave*, people were talking about women's suffrage and the pompadour dress Mrs. Cleveland wore at the reception in the Blue Parlor of the White House. The Curtis family of Cordova, Leseur County, Wisconsin, heard about those things too in 1887 but their own interests were concentrated on something more vital to them. They were going West on a great adventure, to Washington Territory.

It was a desperation move. Johnson Curtis had fought in the Civil War as a private in a Wisconsin regiment to return with ruined health. He became a minister in the United Brethren Church but even this work was too bitterly exhausting. He had a wife and family of four children and no prospects of prosperity. The boys were Ray, twenty-six; Edward S., nineteen, who had been born on a farm near Whitewater, Wisconsin in 1868 and Asahel, thirteen. The daughter, Eva, was seventeen.

Edward had already caught camera fever. His father bought a stereoptican and the boy became fascinated with it. From somewhere came a copy of Wilson's *Quarter of a Century of Photography* and from this tome came inspiration. With two wooden boxes, one fitting into the other, the stereoptican lens in front, he built his own camera. Shortly he was printing the negatives and attempting unsuccessfully to make a paying business of it. When he learned of a job opening in a St. Paul photograph gallery, he managed to make the trip and by assuring the owner he was experienced, he obtained the job. For over a year he worked in the darkroom, printing and coating paper, then was allowed to take a few photographs.

Unable to work, Johnson Curtis knew his only hope lay in a change of scene, one in which he could breathe invigorating sea air. "We must go West," he told Ellen Sheriff Curtis, "to that new country on Puget Sound where the weather is more moderate and life can be easier. The change of outlook will pick up our spirits." Accordingly he took Edward with him on the long trail and settled on a claim of land at Sydney, across Puget Sound from the brash city of Seattle.

At home in Cordova, Ellen Curtis received encouraging letters. "This is fine, invigorating country, but raw and frontier-like. Lots of Indians around and water—water—water. It's rainy and foggy but not cold like there. Everybody is talking about Alaska away up North."

He told the family about the log cabin he and Edward had built, the brick yard he was acquiring and thought hard work was what he needed. S e a t t l e? "They call it the Queen City and talk about its great future although it wasn't very long ago there were Indian attacks on the town. It's over 10,000 and there's a university in the middle of town and hills all around it. Edward says they have telephones—120 of them."

An emigrant sleeping car on the railroad the next spring carried Ellen Curtis and the other children west. They brought their own bedding, sleeping in one half of the car and cooking their meals on a coal stove at the other end. "And it seemed like luxury and going to the end of the world," Eva told her father in the snug warmth before the big fireplace in the Sydney cabin. "Only I didn't see one Indian. Haven't yet even. A lot of mountains. And all those plank sidewalks in Seattle. Do you know, papa, I'll bet the boat that brought us over here was the first big one you ever were on. Here I am, only a young girl and I've sailed on a boat and it's called the *Ellis* and it's dark red."

The bright prospects faded quickly. Edward and his father built another room of hewn timber and the strain told on the sick man. Pneumonia developed and although attended by a doctor from Seattle, Johnson Curtis died. Ellen and her hungry brood were faced with sharp uncertainties in this primitive setting. Yet they "got along." They had vegetables and fruit trees on the homestead, the boys fished and dug clams. Edward cut forest wood to sell and hired himself out to the neighbors, yet always finding time for his camera work.

This "taking pictures" was not always a popular subject in the family. So often distressed for the bare necessities of life, any dalliance or attempt to spend time at some activity that brought in no money or food was considered a capricious and futile waste of time. Yet Edward's mother knew there was something about this picture taking which had a strangle hold on her son.

"Mrs. Summerly needs some spading done over at her place," she would say, doubting that Edward heard her. He was reading a copy of a Seattle newspaper. "You go and see her." Edward would look up, pointing to an item in the paper.

"Look there, mother. That's the ship I took a picture of a month ago. The *George W. Elder*. She runs from San Francisco to Seattle and Alaska. I got set up on the wharf and took some dandy pictures. All right—all right. I'll see what Mrs. Summerly wants."

The incident was further sparked by the fact that the *George W. Elder* was the ship on which he was himself to sail to Alaska some seven years later as official photographer of the Harriman Expedition.

Now every n e w s i g h t on Puget Sound s t i m u l a t e d the imagination of the nineteen-year-old boy with the "camera bug." Steamboats by the hundreds plied the waters. Loggers and their bulls cut great swaths through the timber, Indians trapped and fished and shot harbor seals. And from the meagre scrapings Edward saved money to buy a better camera from a man who needed extra money for a grubstake and trip to the California mines.

It was these Puget Sound Indians who caught most of his interest. Even at twenty-one he realized these deteriorating, fat and lazy Tulalips and Muckleshoots did not represent the stalwart, principled tribesmen the school books told about. And t h e more intrigued Edward was with the toothless old women squatting listlessly in front of rough board shanties, the reckless young bucks tormenting the parched and serried patriarchs, the more he looked beyond them to the days before the white man's interference. Somewhere in this drab front were traces of their former nobility. Would he ever be able to show it to the public?

Admittedly t h e immediate problem was that of making a living, yet the young Curtis believed he could sell prints of his Indian pictures if he applied a bit of artistry. He would make them lifelike yet try to show in the figures a certain respect and dignity —to lend mystery and enchantment to the Nootka squaws who sold baskets on the muddy streets or the Chimakums camped on a sandspit called Ballast Island. To get the right pictures he would approach these people as a friend, work with them as with children and not as curiosities to be exploited.

And Seattle began to notice some unusual Indian pictures in a dingy window on an uphill street—the Imperial Photograph Co. at 1108 Fifth Avenue. Ships from Portland and San Francisco brought travelers who chanced to see Edward Curtis' prints and wanted to send one to the home folks—"You see, Lily, there are Indians out West here but they don't ride horses or shoot buffalo."

Clara Phillips entered ambition's dreams and plans in this year—1892—when Edward was twenty-four. He found in her the girl he wanted to marry. It was the year also he learned Peter Sandstrom, who likewise had come from Cordova and had been an influence in the westward move of the Curtis family, wanted to sell his interest in a small photographic studio in the Rialto Building on Second Avenue. The price would be $150. Did Edward Curtis want to buy it?

He certainly did. And his enthusiasm was so great it flowed over into the purse of a man who could loan $150 on the prospects of profits from the business. It flowed even into the heart of Clara Phillips who became Mrs. Edward S. Curtis. Jokingly the young photographer was later asked: "Which did you marry last year, Ed—Clara or the business?" So attentive was the budding champion of the Indian's cause, he himself sometimes wondered which.

The studio was renamed "Curtis-Guptil," the partner being Thomas H. Guptil, the firm known as "Photographers and Photoengravers." It specialized in portraits of men, women and children. In 1894 the "Guptil" was dropped and in a few years the studio was moved into the Downs Block at 709 Second Avenue.

Buffalo Herd—Apsaroke Country of South Dakota

During this period the man with his own eye and that of the camera trained on the Indians spent three seasons in tribal territory—the first two with the Tulalip north of Seattle, the third with the Blackfeet in Montana.

"My first picture," Curtis was fond of recalling, "was of Princess Angeline, the daughter of Chief Sealth after whom Seattle was named. She was getting old then. Her father had died at Old Man House in 1866, her mother and brother a few years later, another brother, Jim, in 1882. Angeline lived in a little house on the Seattle waterfront. I photographed her digging clams and gave her a dollar. 'More easy work than dig clams,' she told me."

From the best of his accumulated work with the Indians, Curtis made large exhibition prints of three studies—"The Clam Digger," "The Mussel Gatherer" and "Homeward." These were entered in a contest sponsored by the National Photographic Convention and to the great elation of the Curtis clan, won the Grand Prize. As a loan exhibition the pictures toured Europe and other countries for two years, winning prizes and medals wherever shown.

In the meantime destiny approached with glittering brilliance on the ice slope of a glacier. Edward Curtis was a mountaineer with a practical side. He had made several climbing trips into the crevasses and chimneys of Mt. Rainier with a new 14 x 17

20

camera and had sold several prints made from the glass plates. He had become proficient in climbing and with equipment strapped to his back, could cut his way up an ice face, brace and vault with alpenstock. During the second year of these expeditions, he strayed into the col below jagged Little Tahoma and there came upon a lost and despairing, half-starved climbing party.

"An angel must have been brushing his shoulder," as the saying went, for Curtis learned after he got the men into his camp and thawed them out, that they were well-known scientists and government specialists—among them Dr. C. Hart Merriam, Chief of U. S. Biological Survey; Gifford Pinchot, Chief of U. S. Forestry Department and George Bird Grinnell, editor of *Forest and Stream* Magazine. They were members of a government commission and had been climbing the mountain in two groups, by the Longmire and an alternate route. The latter unit had missed its guide points and the men were now eternally in debt to this young and enterprising photographer.

Edward S. C u r t i s was to benefit almost at once f r o m this fortuitous rescue. Before the parties came down the mountain, Grinnell, Merriam and Curtis became well acquainted and this friendship continued through correspondence after the editor and outdoorsman returned East. During the winter the s u b j e c t of a possible expedition north was broached and by spring the discussions had reached the proposal stage.

"Mr. E. H. Harriman," George Bird Grinnell wrote in effect, "is now organizing a party to explore Alaska from a ship. He is the wealthy railroad man—wealthy through manipulation of railroad stock—who now believes in doing something in a scientific way. He has given Mr. Merriam and myself great latitude in securing competent people to support his project and Edward, we want you to go along as photographer."

The man was overwhelmed at the honor and the opportunity such a trip afforded. At first he could only believe it was fanciful talk but facts began to pound the fancy into reality. Twenty-five scientists were now chosen to study the natives and glaciers. The steamer *George W. Elder* had been chartered. Sailing date was May 30 from Seattle. There was no dodging the issue—Edward S. Curtis had been selected as Official Photographer and he was to have an assistant!

Originally, the "official photographer" learned, the expedition had been planned as a summer cruise by members of the Harriman family and their friends, and on which Dr. D. G. Elliot, Curator of Zoology at Chicago's Field Museum, was to hunt Kodiak bear. Then through the influence of the Washington Academy of Science plans were extended. Finally, after a conference at Washington with Dr. C. Hart Merriam, a full-fledged scientific effort had been worked out.

The Harriman party left New York by train May 23, 1899, and met the western people in Seattle, sailing on the *George W. Elder* as scheduled, May 30. On the guest list were three artists and twenty-five men of science, many of their names impressive to the wide-eyed Edward Curtis. He found J o h n Burroughs, eminent ornithologist and author; Henry Gannett of the U. S. Geological Survey; John Muir, naturalist, scholar and author, whose particular study now was glaciers. He was interested in Dr. Merriam's biological knowledge but, above all, his discovered friend and counselor was George Bird Grinnell, whom he soon learned was known as the "Father of the Blackfoot People," the same fascinating tribe Curtis had visited and studied in Montana the year before.

With his assistant, D. G. Inverarity, of Seattle, Edward Curtis made over five thousand photographs on the Harriman Expedition and the two-month, nine-thousand-mile voyage made a profound impression upon him. He was never content, during the following years, until he returned to photograph the Alaskan natives and Arctic Circle Eskimos, which he did in 1927. Constantly recurring to him, as he was camped in Navaho or Apsaroke country, were the shipboard talks with Grinnell as the steamer felt her way through the "opal, flame-riven mists" of the northern seas. It was then the pattern was formed for the Curtis future, although at the time he saw it only as his first opportunity to live with the Indians, learn their ways from a master teacher, then put some photographic ideas to work.

"My young friend," Grinnell had said, "I have been with the Blackfeet for some months every year over the past twenty. I love and respect them, and they me. They have made me an honorary chief and have given me a place of special consideration in their ceremonial lodge—in the direct center of the great tribal circle during the Sun Dance encampment. Curtis—I want you to come there with me next year. Your compassionate attitude toward the Indians will help them. I can help you gain their confidence and they will cooperate in helping you make some fine pictures."

It was arranged.

CHAPTER THREE

Focus on the Future

AS Edward Marshall wrote in the May, 1912, issue of *Hampton's* Magazine, it was the mere desire to excel in the photography of nature which first started Edward S. Curtis at work among the Indians. He wished to touch them with his camera and here they were, ready at his hand. Here they were, the Blackfoot group of the Piegan tribe in northern Montana extending on up into Canada. And here he was mingling with them on their reservation, beside their campfires, in the dim shadows of their tent lodges, kneeling with them in the tall grass of the hunting grounds, bowing in humility to the swift-running rivers.

Curtis was here by the grace of his mentor, George Bird Grinnell, and as the man had said, he was accepted as the true friend of the true friend of the Blackfeet. And as he watched, with the wonder of all the ages, the wild and terrible self-torture of the Sun Dance, knowing he was being indulged in rare privilege, his mind formed inspired thoughts.

What he was seeing had been viewed by few white men, and with proficiency in his camera work, he could perhaps do what no white man could ever do again. This Indian was vanishing, dying almost before his eyes. Yet if he worked fast enough over the next few years he could catch a comprehensive picture of the passing pageant before eternity swallowed it. He let his ideas flow out to the receptive ears of his friend.

"I don't know how many tribes there are west of the Missouri, Bird—maybe a hundred. But I want to make them live forever—in a sort of history by photographs. No, I mean in both photography and words, if I can write them. And if I live long enough. You and I know, and of course everybody does who thinks of it, the Indians of North America are vanishing. They've crumbled from their pride and power into pitifully small numbers, painful poverty and sorry weakness. There won't be anything left of them in a few generations and it's tragedy—a national tragedy. Thinking people must realize this.

"So I want to produce an irrefutable record of a race doomed to extinction—to show this Indian as he was in his normal, noble life so people will know he was no debauched vagabond but a man of proud stature and noble heritage.

"Bird—I believe I can do something about it. I have some ability. I can live with

23

these people, get their confidence, understand them and photograph them in all their natural attitudes. It's such a big dream I can't see it all, so many tribes to visit, so many strange people. But I can start— and sell prints of my pictures as I go along. I'm a poor man but I've got my health, plenty of steam and something to work for."

Grinnell, the editor, caught the Curtis enthusiasm. Although realizing his friend's genius had already found expression in photographs this far, he was also aware that he himself had been of some influence in this vision. He encouraged the idea at once, understanding the magnitude of the project and its full importance. He agreed to help all he could and get others to accept the idea. And in the few days remaining of their close association he brought out many points Curtis should cover in his research. Five years later, after the resulting photographs had gained international significance, he wrote of his experiences with the man who had made them.

"While Mr. Curtis is first of all an artist, he does not think solely of his art. His mind is broad enough to see the humanity of his subjects and the importance of learning about them all that can be learned. He realizes the work's scientific value, and not content with making these beautiful and faithful records of the old-time life, with all its varied round of travel and social intercourse and ceremonial, he feels that pictures alone are not enough. They tell the story of that life in part but they require some explanation, and as each picture represents some state or action, the reason and cause for what the picture shows, should also be explained and recorded. Therefore, besides making his pictures, Curtis is gathering from each tribe he visits all that he can which relates to its customs, beliefs and ceremonials, and is thus accumulating information of great value in itself but of still greater value as a supplement to his pictures.

"I have never seen pictures relating to Indians which for fidelity to nature, combined with artistic feeling, can compare with these photographs by Curtis. Today they are of high scientific and artistic value. What will they be a hundred years from now, when the Indians shall have utterly vanished from the face of the earth? The pictures will show to the man of that day who and what were his predecessors in the land. They will tell how the Indian lived, what were his beliefs, how he carried himself in the various operations of life, and they will tell it as no word picture can ever tell it.

"The pictures speak for themselves and the artist who made them is devoted to his work. To accomplish it he has exchanged ease, comfort, home life, for the hardest kind of work, frequent and long-continued separations from his family, the wearing toil of traveling through difficult regions, and finally the heartbreaking struggle of winning over to his purpose primitive men, to whom ambition, time and money mean nothing, but to whom a dream or a cloud in the sky, or a bird flying across the trail from the wrong direction has some deep significance."

Ten days after leaving Grinnell and the Blackfeet, Curtis was in Arizona making his judicious advances to the Hopi Indians in their sun-cured cliff houses. He had made a quick return to Seattle for a visit with his wife and children. His brother, Ashahel, who had gone with the Gold Rush to Alaska, had returned to open his own studio, and the Curtis Studio business was now carried on by A. F. Muhr and associates. This arrangement, Edward knew, would have to continue for the time being as he was embarked on a long and involved project closer to his heart.

There were many difficulties in the way, not the least of which was money. It was a costly procedure to transport himself, cameras and equipment by train and wagon into the tribal wilds. Yet meagre funds were provided from the business and he plunged ahead with his customary dash and verve. At thirty-four the man was bursting with energy. He was big, with more than six feet of rugged frame and he drove the huge body with relentless force.

For now he had a new field of life work, an historical duty that was virgin in its opportunities. He was going down a path never traveled by artist or photographer as he would travel it. He was to reproduce the American Indian in his native dress, portray him at home in tipi and hogan, with his squaw and p a p o o s e s, his horse, gun and trappings, in canoes and on the hunt—to depict the man and his country together with blankets, bows, arrows—and tell the full story of the Indian.

Yet he had not begun to surmount the greatest difficulties. The long traverse, rides over dusty tracks in the desert, sleeping in a blanket on bare ground, eating the coarse, dry foods—these were nothing in the face of the big problem—how to overcome the Indian prejudice, superstition and suspicion of a prying, white man stranger.

However, Edward Curtis had a great many helpful gifts. With all his physical force and eagerness, he had patience and an understanding heart. He needed the tribesman's confidence, his friendship, yet he was willing to wait for it while smiling and talking about the sun, the moon, the wind—those things the people understood. Day by day, the hostile and aloof attitudes softened. And once confidences were exchanged, Curtis never abused them.

There were over-alert and over-suspicious white men too—the government agents who guarded their charges and rights zealously and many times selfishly. Many were wary of all encroachment, suspecting spies sent out from Washington or fearing official wrath to fall on their heads if they allowed this photographer to take pictures on their sacred preserves. Yet in the end the disarming personality melted their bold fronts and they began to respect his ideas and the courage he displayed in meeting Indians on their own ground and native level. Of this first concerted effort to photograph the Hopis as they lived, Curtis said:

"I was enlightened many times by the readiness of the people to tell me what I wanted to know but it usually required days and weeks of casual conversation before I could get through their deep-seated superstitions and secretive beliefs to get a glimpse of their inner selves. Long and serious study was necessary before I could understand the meaning of their esoteric rites and ceremonies.

"It may seem difficult to photograph wild animals in their dens or haunts but I found it much more difficult to get the pictures of Indians I had in mind. If a certain man of the tribe does not take kindly to my camera to the extent of allowing a white man to pose him, nothing on earth will change his mind nor will he grant an expression for the good photograph.

"I found many times, especially where Indians were congregated in an area remote from modern ways, the chiefs would decide, when they learned about my mission, that I was not wanted as a visitor and I was told this in a few words of broken English that left no doubt as to the meaning. To argue the point was well nigh useless, for as a rule, Indian logic is apart from the American's and it is very difficult to grasp the reason behind the refusal.

"Many of my early experiences were amusing, many tragic. My tents have been blown away and my whole outfit almost flooded away in a torrent of rain. I have lost my way in the mountains, all but drowned when my canoe overturned in a swift river. On my very first expedition, my mule stumbled and fell from a cliff, smashing many of my precious plates so that I was forced to return to camp and do the job over again.

"My mission? Yes, it was a mission and I felt like a missionary must often feel. I was working alone against a great array of odds and advice from people whose judgment in most things I respected highly. I would never get the pictures I had in my idyllic imagination. I would never get money enough to carry on this ambitious project. I wouldn't sell enough pictures and I couldn't keep on taking them and expect other people to donate the cost. The advice was free but so was turning my back on it.

"I made one resolve in those early days—that the pictures should be made according to the best of modern methods and of a size that the face might be studied as the Indians' own flesh. And above all, none of these pictures would admit anything which betokened civilization, whether in an article of dress or landscapes or objects on the ground. These pictures were to be transcriptions for future generations that they might behold the Indian as nearly lifelike as possible as he moved about before he ever saw a paleface or knew there was anything human or in nature other than what he himself had seen."

Edward Curtis got glimpses into the workings of the primitive mind and far more. Under the full moon of August, the mesas still warm from the scorching sun, he witnessed his first Hopi Snake Dance as a privileged spectator. It was a weird, mysterious rite, symbolizing the prayer for rain and a bountiful corn harvest. Then after it was ended he exacted promises from the Snake Priests for photographs to be taken the next day.

From one Indian camp to another, Curtis tramped with the excitement of exploration and conquest. Along the banks of the Gila and Colorado Rivers, across the hot sands of the Mohave desert, over the purple hills and through the endless reaches of mesquite, cottonwood and cactus—he searched for even a little welcome and was sometimes rewarded with much.

Once in those first days of trial and error, he sent for his wife, son Harold who was then about eleven, and daughters Florence, aged seven, and Beth, nine. He met their train at Gallup, New Mexico and took them over the thin, dusty track in a big covered wagon. It was a thrilling, new experience for them, a trying one for him.

The first night's camp was at St. Michaels, near the Days' trading post. Their eldest son Charlie, who had lived with the Navahos all his life, was to be guide and interpreter, the ultimate destination Canon de Chelly. The party was several days traveling through the canyon, the heavy sand making progress slow.

A camp was made in a verdant oasis of cottonwoods and cornfields belonging to the Navahos. A burro was secured for the children to ride and they spent much time digging in a nearby cliff dwelling for Indian artifacts. Although it was forbidden ground they were not stopped, the natives watching them closely to see they did not desecrate "the place of the old ones."

Late one afternoon, Edward Curtis spoke to the others in a guarded voice which carried with it caution and alarm. There were no Indians in camp and all were told to stay together, as close to him as possible. Then sounds of Navaho singing grew louder, the weird chants echoing and reverberating between the high canyon walls. Curtis and the guide moved off to a tree clump, the latter conveying the information

Curtis Trail Wagon in Navaho Country   Curtis is seated on wagon gate at right of young white guide Charlie Day. Girls are daughters Florence (left) and Beth. Navaho interpreter stands at right.

that a woman was sick, in child labor for a long time, a medicine man placing the cause of it on the camp of the white people.

"Mr. Curtis," the guide said solemnly, "we are in some trouble. We dare not leave here until that baby arrives. We should not stay here but—just pray to God both the baby and woman live."

On and on went the haunting monotony of the medicine chant. Curtis and the guide rode out a short distance and suddenly returned with orders to strike the camp. Tents and equipment were hurriedly piled into the wagon and the horses driven hard along the desert sands. Curtis had been told the baby was born and the mother better and no one in the party felt a greater lift than he did. In later years he said it was one of the most unnerving experiences of his life—the realization that he was helpless to protect the others and that all their lives had been at the mercy of an Indian medicine man's whims. For days afterward, he said he could hear Charlie Day's ominous words—"Just pray to God both the baby and mother live."

The experience proved valuable to researcher Curtis in his dealings with the Navahos and made a profound impression on the children in their formative years. Curtis never took the family on such trips again although on various occasions he included single members.

The Apaches. Curtis found them passively removed from his inquiring mind yet particularly intriguing in light of his sketchy reading of their history and purported origin. "As I fraternized with them," he explained later, "and my approach was necessarily diffident, I saw that what I had read as facts were only theories and one contradicted the other. Linguistically the Apaches belong to the great Athapascan family which, according to most published reports, seems to have its origin in the Far North where many tribes of that family still live, and that the Apaches—and Navahos—appeared in this Southwest mesa country about the time America was discovered.

"Yet as I picked up bits of Apache and Navaho legends of creation I found no hint of origin in any other place than this region. The history and legendary lore of the Indian are passed down from generation to generation and it seemed incredible that all trace of a migration from the North would be lost within a period of some 400 years. I wanted to learn more and get at the truth.

"Because of his cunning, his fearlessness and long resistance to subjection both by the missionary and the government under whose dominion he lived but to which he has never fully acceded, the name Apache has become infamous to us. Some of this is due also to his being the scourge of the peaceable Indians in nearby territory and for about 300 years a menace to the brave colonists who settled within his striking range. So except for meagre records and a few tales told by army officers, the Apache's inner life has been a closed book. I proposed to do something to open it.

"I approached them with simulated indifference. I asked no questions and indicated no interest in matters beyond externals. By observation of their daily life, I learned they were devoutly religious. The men were up at dawn and if pools or streams were available, they bathed that their bodies be acceptable to the gods. Each man isolated himself and greeted the rising sun in fervent invocation. Shrines were visited secretly, offerings and supplications made.

"In all this I realized that if I asked a single question or displayed curiosity as to their devotional rites, I would defeat my purpose. It would have been fatal to have asked my interpreter any question along this line.

"My apparent indifference was so convincing that at the mescal harvest and the ceremonial firing of the roasting pit they went on with the proceedings as though no alien was present. The fire to the gods was lighted with the fire sticks as the divine ones had taught them. The sacred pollen—spirit of fecundity—was scattered to the gods of the four winds, to the earth and the sky. In their prayers I heard the names of the divine ones constantly repeated until I knew the names of the gods of the east, west, south, north, the sky and earth, but I had no key to this vast storehouse of primitive belief.

"My primary idea was to secure pictures. I employed parties to go with me on long trips into the mountains. In my assumed nonchalant indifference I managed to include in the parties men with wives and children, widows with or without children, medicine men and men of the common average. Had the medicine men dreamed that I possessed a real questioning thought, nothing could have induced them to join the party. But no—I was just a sucker furnishing the food and paying for the privilege. Medicine men went on with their devotions, husbands kept rendezvous with widows, wives and widows came stealthily to me with their daughters expounding their virtues and charms and insisted that it was not good that a man live for himself only

28

and care for his own camp. Some of the offered maidens needed no sales argument and I sometimes wonder now if scruples were justified. At least I had the satisfaction of knowing I had no part in the amalgamation of the races.

"The Navaho tribe, second only to the Sioux in numbers, has been the least affected by civilizing influences. They are the American Bedouins, the principal human touch in the great plateau-desert region of our Southwest. They acknowledged no superior, pay allegiance to no chief. Their activities center in their flocks and small farms and they ask nothing of the government save to be let alone.

"Their reservation of more than 14,000 square miles is the desert-plateau region of northern Arizona and New Mexico. Its mesas and low mountains are sparsely covered with pinon and cedar and in the higher levels are beautiful forests of pine. Back and forth in all parts of this vast region the Navahos drive their flocks. At the season when the slight rainfall produces even scant pasturage on the desert plains the flocks are pastured there, but as the grass becomes seared by the summer sun they are taken into the mountain shade. Then as the deep winter snows come, the sheep and goats are driven down to the wooded mesas where there is little snow but an abundance of food. And so, year in and year out, the flocks slowly drift back and forth from plain to mesa and mesa to mountain.

"After many days of trial and tribulation I was able to photograph their Yebichai ceremony. This is a nine-day ritual for the curing of disease of l o n g standing. With the Navaho people all ceremonies are termed 'sings' and the medicine men, 'singers.' Superior to these medicine men are the thirteen gods of Navaho mythology—eight male and five female—and of these the principal ones are Na-Ya-Nez—Ga-Ni or the Elder Brother, To-Bad-Zis-Tsi-Ni, or the Younger Brother, and Ta-Na-Nelly—the three forming a trinity.

"The distinctive feature of the Yebichai ceremony is the sweat administered to the patient for four successive days. The entire ceremony is enacted around a sort of sacred hut or primitive temple, called 'hogan,' and the sweat is given to the patient in the open outside it. Compared with the Yebichai sweat the Turkish bath is a chilly affair.

"On the second day of the ceremony a shallow hole is dug in the earth about the length of the patient's body and red hot embers are placed within, covered with spruce boughs and wet down so they will not burn. The patient is stripped of his clothing, wrapped tightly in a blanket and laid on the boughs. At the end of about twenty minutes the blanket is unrolled enough to give the patient a drink of herb medicine, which no doubt keeps him from going unconscious. After another twenty minutes, an effort is made to frighten away any remaining illness by men wearing hideous masks to represent various deities. They rush upon the patient with unearthly hoots and yells which cause him to faint or fall into an hysterical fit. This curing process cannot be complete until the patient pays the medicine man and the cost of feeding the entire multitude for nine days."

CHAPTER FOUR

Honor in High Places

T HE hunter is home from the hills," began a Seattle newspaper article when Edward S. Curtis settled back into studio work in the late fall of 1904. "He brings with him the result of many months spent in the field which to him is the Indian camp. He has become a dedicated hunter with a fine talent, that of taking masterful photographs of the natives. His latest acquisitions to be viewed at his Downs Block studio are of the mountain and desert tribes of the Southwest."

Seattle was not unappreciative of the Curtis talent. He had many friends in the city, among others—Sam Hill, cousin of railroader Jim Hill and associated with him; Colonel Alden J. Blethen and son Joe, Thomas Noyes, Fred Sanders, Amos Brown, the Stimsons and in later years James F. Douglas. They purchased prints, sent others in to see them and aided the work in many other ways.

But Curtis had brought home over a thousand negatives of rare and revealing quality. The studio staff had worked long hours in the darkroom to bring out the full beauty of them while Edward made camera experiments and refinements. With all this he failed to see the world beating a path to his door. He knew there would have to be a greater effort made to distribute the pictures in order to raise the funds to carry on his project.

There were occasional orders from other cities. And now came Erastus Brainard to him with a suggestion. He lived in Washington, D.C. where he acted as lobbyist for the State of Washington. He thought it a good idea to take a dozen of the Curtis pictures back East with him and since President Theodore Roosevelt had shown an interest in Indians, perhaps he would like one or two of these photographs. It was a gesture of some importance, Curtis realized, but he could not hold any great hope for immediate good. He made a selection and thought little more about the matter.

He was fully aware of the bitter truth that Seattle was immature as a city, too busy doing things to indulge in such aesthetic pursuits as buying photographs like his. It was growing fast. The Gold Rush to the Yukon had brought the country's attention to Puget Sound, its watery wonderland and moderate climate. But the people who migrated here from Michigan, Minnesota, Wisconsin and the Dakotas were farmers, loggers and the normal sifting of adventurers and opportunists. There were just not enough people of settled habits and proper perspective to afford beauty on their walls.

"Look here, Ed," a friend in the steamship business said one day. "I think some of those pictures of yours are the most wonderful things I ever saw. But who the hell else thinks so in this rough, bruising, frontier country? Oh, sure—there are some and we're going to find out how many. Here's what I'm going to do. I'm going to hire a hall and you're going to fill it full of stuff. If you want to pay the rent, all right. If you don't—I will. That's just to show you I'm not mad at you but just a little bit disgusted at the rubes around here."

Edward Curtis did not give a formal talk at that first exhibition in Christensen's Hall which opened on December 2, 1904. It was a surprising success without words for the photographs spoke for themselves. Each tribe was accorded its own space and the patrons could make brief studies of the native life and ceremonies. In eloquent phrase a newspaper article assessed the occasion.

"Long since the artistic merits had been recognized but never before was this value so fully established as by a study of the work in such overwhelming numbers. It was bewildering to find that artistic instinct even in such things, insignificant in themselves, as an Apache and other still life studies in which some baskets or other articles are tossed together seemingly in a careless manner. The touch of the artist is everywhere visible and nothing seems too trivial for his careful consideration. Some of the pictures, had they come from the easel of an artist painter, would be considered marvelous creations, so thoroughly does everything harmonize. Even the skies seem to bend to the will of his genius to complete atmospheric effects that make the pictures simply wonderful.

"As pictures, a great many will enjoy lasting recognition while they still remain important individually in their respective series. Take the 'Three Chiefs,' so strongly typical of the endless rolling prairies of Montana, the eyes of the strong central group scanning the encircling distant horizon, monarchs of the domain. It is almost pathetic when we realize that the horizon is continually narrowing as civilization, in its irresistible approach, closes in on them. This picture is so remarkable in its l i n e s of composition that we marvel how the artistic requirements could be accomplished with the camera.

" 'Getting Water' is easily the gem of the Apache series, without disputing the merits of many others. The lines of the bank, the crouching figure of the squaw dipping water from the creek and the horses on the bank make a very pleasing composition, while the filmy trees in the background aid in giving tone and atmosphere. There are indeed so many fine accomplishments here that it seems impossible to do them justice. 'The Vanishing Race' with its ghostly figures like shadows in the night possesses a haunting mysticism rarely found in pictures.

"Had Shakespeare ever seen the study 'In the Canyon de Chelly' we might understand how he could cause Hamlet to say—'What a piece of work is a man! How noble in reason! How infinite in faculty! . . in form and moving, how expressive and admirable! . . . . in action, how like an angel! . . . . in apprehension, how like a god! . . . the beauty of the world! . . . . the paragon of animals! And yet, to me, what is this quintessence of dust?' "

In appreciation of this first modest exhibition, Curtis was guest of honor at a dinner held by members of Seattle's Rainier Club, of which he himself was one. More than a hundred lantern slides were shown and as he explained them he was asked to detail the great difficulty of getting the pictures. When the neighbor city of Portland, Oregon, read the dispatches, Curtis was invited by his mountaineer friends, the Mazamas, to make a public address.

"His marvelous portraits of Indians," said the *Oregonian* of January 15, 1905, "illustrating the vanishing race in all its ancient glory, is not only a new revelation in art which appeals to all lovers of the picturesque and beautiful but also a study of Indian customs and character in all its most subtle and fascinating form. It is surely an educational work of unique and remarkable value which should be enjoyed by all public school pupils, teachers, students of American history and the public generally."

And now with this historical and artistic value being recognized to a limited extent locally, the man himself was greatly encouraged to test the tastes of the effete East. After correspondence with the Washington Academy of Science and with the aid of E. H. Harriman, an exhibition was set up in the Washington Club of that capital city.

All of Curtis' apprehension fled suddenly in a rush of acclaim. In the words of the press, the evening was a "sensation. Not only are photographers and artists discussing its merits with special reference to his achievements in the new process of color printing, but prominent scientific men are enthusiastic in the work Edward S. Curtis has undertaken, namely, the photographic record of all the Indian tribes in the western half of the country."

With such a response in erudite circles, Edward Curtis felt warmly gratified. He had emerged from obscurity and found his work admired and valued. It is probable he reassessed his own worth and the confidence that came with acceptance was added to his personal drive and ambition. The members of the Washington Club were fashionable, intelligent women. Yet he did not bask in their recognition, like a matinee idol, but rather felt more restless than ever, more eager to "get on with the job." This could not be for a time, however. There were more talks to make, other people to see.

The exhibit moved now to the Cosmos Club in the historic old home of Dolly Madison and the scientist members responded as society had, the club purchasing a number of prints for its richly tapestried walls. Curtis was invited to give an informal talk at the home of Gifford Pinchot, chief of the forestry bureau and to lecture at the Washington Academy of Science. And then came two occurrences which brought further prominence and signaled the giant step into the future.

The first was a news event, a visitation of Indians from the western nations during the inauguration of Theodore Roosevelt, who had succeeded to the presidency upon the assassination of William McKinley and had then been reelected. After paying their respects to the "Great White Father" in the White House, fifteen Crow, Omaha and Pawnee men visited the Curtis exhibit, now moved to Morry's Art Gallery.

In another Indian group was the Apache chief, Geronimo, captured by General Miles, now in Washington to plead for his people. Edward Curtis had been invited by Francis Leupp, Commissioner of Indian Affairs, to photograph the assemblage on the White House lawn. There was a drizzle of rain and as he brought his camera forward he saw a tall figure wrapped in a bright red robe awaiting his approach. Drawing near he was greeted by a friendly smile on the gnarled old face of his friend Geronimo. The Indian pulled him within the embrace of his arm, and w r a p p i n g the red blanket around both of them, proceeded toward the presidential group as a pair.

Meeting President Roosevelt was one of the great moments of Curtis' life. He

President Theodore Roosevelt as photographed by Edward Curtis

shook the strong hand, saw the virile face expand into the characteristic smile, heard the hearty voice boom: "Delighted to know you, Mr. Curtis. I have heard of you and your work through the Harrimans and Dr. Merriam. And I wish I knew as much about Indians as you do."

The second memorable event was another kind of visitation. Among the luminaries at the Curtis exhibit was a visitor from New York, Mrs. E. H. Harriman, who brought with her a friend, Mrs. Douglas Robinson, sister of the President. They purchased Indian prints and established ties of friendship which were to pull Edward Curtis up to further heights and assure the continuation of his work.

New York! And a letter. It was addressed to Mr. E. H. Harriman, 120 Broadway, and Edward Curtis read it with an excitement he felt only once again in his long and active life. The ballroom of the Waldorf-Astoria Hotel with its velour-draped walls and soft lighting was thronged with the rich, famous and idly curious. The man they had come to meet was feeling the absurd unreality of the whole scene when he felt a light tap on his arm. He turned to see a hand holding a cream-colored envelope with the words "White House, Washington, D.C." richly printed on the deckled flap. Mrs. Harriman smiled mischievously.

"I think you'll be interested in this. It was sent to my husband. Would you like to read it?"

"Should I read other people's letters?" Curtis quipped.

"Oh, it's quite all right, Mr. Curtis," the lady assured him. "I must confess my husband sent me here today."

Already filled with gratitude for what the Harrimans had done for him, Curtis read the letter with a deep sense of humility. And as he read he knew the impetus which the letter would give his work would carry it far. It was very often true that

33

success depended upon "knowing the right people," although he disliked the phrase and its implications. Even great achievements could go unheralded if power and influence were not available to bring them to the attention of the public. He felt most fortunate and expressed these sentiments to Mrs. Harriman. The letter read:

My dear Mr. Harriman,

I am pleased that Mr. Curtis is exhibiting his really marvelous collection of Indian photographs in New York. Not only are Mr. Curtis' photos genuine works of art but they deal with some of the most picturesque phases of the old-time American life that is now passing away. I esteem it a matter of real moment that for our good fortune Mr. Curtis should have had the will and the power to preserve, as he has preserved in his pictures, this strange and beautiful, and now vanishing, life.

Hoping that his exhibit will have the success it deserves, I am,

Sincerely yours,

THEODORE ROOSEVELT

The exhibit did have the success it deserved but not before the artist suffered grave doubts and confusion. He had agreed to bring the pictures to New York at Mrs. Douglas Robinson's urging and had subsequently made arrangements with the management of the Waldorf-Astoria. Now he learned the cost would be $1,300 and he did not have it. He went on with the program under a heavy cloud of worry.

On the second day of the showing as he was making an inspection, he saw white cards had been attached to many of the pictures. The words "Sold to" had been hand-written on them followed by names which marched regally out of the "400" . . . Mrs. Jack Morgan, Mrs. Jay Gould, Mrs. Frederick Vanderbilt, Mrs. Stuyvesant Fish and— Mrs. Douglas Robinson. She had proved her worth as a patroness. The sale of the pictures more than met the bill.

"We are just waking up here in America," one New York art critic was quoted as saying after he had viewed the Curtis Indian prints, "to appreciating the big interests of our country and to a sense of cherishing our original greatness. We are painting our plains, protecting our forests, creating our game preserves and at last, although not saving the existence of the North American Indian, the most picturesque, roving people on earth, we are making and preserving records of them from an historical, scientific and artistic point of view.

"We as a nation are not doing this but one man, an American, an explorer, an artist with a camera, has conceived and is carrying into execution the gigantic idea of making complete photographic and text records of the North American Indian so far as they exist in a primitive condition today. If Mr. Curtis lives and keeps his health for ten years, he will have accumulated material for the greatest artistic and historical work in American ethnology ever conceived."

Such glowing tribute sent desire burning. When the Waldorf exhibit ended, Edward Curtis shipped his trophies west to the Lewis and Clark Fair being held in Portland, Oregon, and hied himself to the Indian country. When winter came he was again on the east coast with more pictures. An article on the Curtis work by his friend George Bird Grinnell had meanwhile appeared in *Scribner's* M a g a z i n e and opened many new avenues of appreciation. In contrast to his advent of the year previous, Edward Curtis was now welcomed and accepted as the dedicated photo-historian as well as champion of the vanishing race.

CHAPTER FIVE

Bright Light
for Ambition

Mr. Edward S. Curtis of Seattle," wrote Gilbert H. Grosvenor in a general letter, dated January 27, 1906, to members of the National Geographic Society, "gave illustrated talks to the Society in Washington in the winter of 1905 and again this month. On each occasion he had an audience of over one thousand people. I have never seen a more enthusiastic reception given to any lecturer. On each occasion he showed about a hundred and seventy pictures, each of them different, each of them applauded. His Indian portraits and pictures of Western and Southern scenery are unique and marvelous beyond description."

The acclaim was loud and clear in every eastern city. To Boston's Garo Studio, where the Indian picture exhibit was held, came successful men of affairs, elegant women interested in photography, the sciences and history of western life. Artists and faculty members of Harvard, Boston University and the Massachusetts Institute of Technology paid their respects to the Indian prints and the man who had made them.

When the exhibit moved to St. Botolph's Club, the Boston *Transcript* reported the large attendance. "He has brought out, in defiance of the mechanical limitations of his medium, so much of the human element, the individuality, the pathos and even the majesty of the aboriginal types."

In Pittsburgh, the Carnegie Art Gallery glowed with the Curtis pictures and exclamations of praise. Said the Pittsburgh *Leader*: "Anyone who will look at this Indian collection will say at once that the man who made it knows nature and loves it. The wonder is, how can one, with a camera, show so much of nature and the primitive life, and while he is wondering at the art achievement, he hears the maker say—'You know the value of this work is as a document in history and ethnology.'"

Edward Curtis was riding the crests yet he did not lift his feet off the ground. All the prominence and glare of publicity had a sobering effect. Ever since the two memorable weeks with Bird Grinnell on the Blackfoot reservation, when he had conceived his plan for a picture-text history of the Western Indian, he had realized it was a big job. Now with this glimmer of success, he felt a definite obligation to the public swelling all around him and this had the effect of magnifying the importance and size of the project to such a point that it seemed utterly impossible to do all he wanted to do. And the biggest of the problems was that eternally nagging one—money.

Since his growing sheaf of prints remained in the East, he had opened a studio in New York which brought in some extra revenue, but this must be used to cover his increased living expenses. The Seattle studio could not be counted on for more than enough to keep the family. The great demand was for field work costs and it was a constant worry.

After his second exhibit at the Waldorf-Astoria in January, 1906, a White House secretary informed him the President was going on vacation and would like to see him, take time to look at all the Indian pictures he could bring and discuss the whole work. An appointment was made and for the second time he almost held his breath as he talked to Theodore Roosevelt. But this time the ice was broken. Edward S. Curtis was current news and Teddy was a patron of his. They relaxed in the President's study.

"That afternoon did more to spur me on to greater effort," Curtis said later, "than any other influence could have. The President would study a dozen of the Indian pictures, then lean back and talk about them, about his own beliefs concerning the Indians, his honest opinions of this photograph and that and the whole scope of the work. His deep intellectual grasp of the project was greater than even I had envisioned. The fervor of his encouragement inspired me more than anything anyone had ever said."

The conference lasted over two hours and at the end of it, Theodore Roosevelt doubled his big fist and struck the table emphatically.

"Curtis—you have started a colossal job but it must be completed. You're the only man who can do it and I will give you every assistance possible."

He hesitated as though with sudden thought. Then: "I know one of the big problems is money. It will cost thousands to get what you're working for and the public should pay for part of it. It's a project for the public. You have great talent. It should be subsidized."

"It's true, Mr. President, it's such a big job the cost of it scares me a little. That's no secret. But yet I can't be beholden to anybody, nor can I expect rich people to be heated up on Indians the way I am. I had thought the Smithsonian Institution or Washington Academy of Science would go along but there is no word from that quarter."

"Well, I have one. Why don't you see Mr. Morgan?"

"J. P. Morgan—the financier?"

"That's exactly it—the financier. He's a great philanthropist when he thinks the cause is worthy."

Curtis was astounded at his own audacity, that he would approach J. Pierpont Morgan for money. But as TR talked on and the interview came to an end, the brashness faded into logic. This was certainly a worthy cause. Why shouldn't Morgan and his money help? By afternoon he had convinced himself there was an outside chance the Morgan Foundation could and would come to the rescue. Before evening an appointment was made.

Being a man of staunch purpose, Edward Curtis showed and felt all confidence when he strode into the House of Morgan and the teak-panelled private office of this fabulously rich man. The banker did not rise, smiled curtly and spoke bluntly. Curtis towered above him—a handsome man, distinguished by his neatly trimmed Van Dyke. A western giant, Morgan may have thought.

"You wish to interest me in your Indian pictures? I have knowledge of them, Mr. Curtis. Very good, indeed."

Hope surely began to fade and confidence edge to the thin side, as the caller detailed his appeal. There was no interest reflected in the shrewd eyes, no motion of response in the rough, red face. Curtis went on, explaining his work, outlining his plans, mentioning impressive names of people who were urging him on.

"The project, Mr. Morgan, will take 15 more years and cost thousands more than I will ever be able to supply. I have the time, the ambition, the ability, the friendship of the Indian—everything but enough money."

Morgan touched his bulbous nose about which he was so sensitive. "I have the money, Mr. Curtis, and many requests for the use of it, but I don't believe it would be feasible for me to back such a project however commendable."

The assembly line pressure pushed at Curtis' disappointment—the people waiting outside, the financier's impatience for the interview to end. But the caller had not accepted dismissal yet. Inwardly rebelling at being forced to plead with this iron will, he snatched up his portfolio and spread it open under Morgan's nose. He turned three or four prints over to expose the soft, sepia tones of a Mohave girl with the eyes of an animal.

"That is one of President Roosevelt's favorites," he declared with a defiant smile. "And here is the 'Vanishing Race' which symbolizes my whole work—sets the pace, as it were."

Morgan had ceased to fidget and his pudgy hands were leafing through other prints. They did not stop until the last one lay face down. Then he allowed a faint smile to flicker across his face. It was quickly removed.

"This may be the third or fourth time in my life," he said, almost with apology, "that I have changed my mind after once making it up. I am fascinated with these pictures. I believe I was hasty in my decision. Mr. Curtis—I will aid your work. My staff will work out the details with you. Thank you. Now—others are waiting."

The acceptance was not as barefaced as it might have been. In an aura of exultation, Curtis folded the portfolio and voicing his profound thanks and assurance of the work's success, started for the door. The dry, unemotional words of the financier halted him.

"I want to see these in a set of books, the handsomest ever published."

Edward Curtis recalled few details of the days that followed but realized they fled like startled lemmings. The press saw to it the people were fully informed. The New York, Boston and Washington newspapers carried bright dispatches which were picked up by lesser journals over the country, with such headlines as:

MORGAN MONEY TO KEEP INDIANS FROM OBLIVION
Great Photographic Series—Eskimos
Too To Be Pictured In Daily Tasks
And In Their Ceremonies

The details of Edward S. Curtis' plans were described in the announcement that a gift of $75,000 would be made by J. Pierpont Morgan, to be paid in five yearly installments of $15,000. Promise became reality, and banking his first Morgan check, the artist left the drawing room for the sagebrush hills with the firm knowledge that the one big obstacle in his ambitious program had been surmounted. However, he left behind him, in Washington and Sagamore Hill, the baronial home of the Roosevelts, a set of unfinished circumstances.

The President's admiration for Edward Curtis was genuine and when, later in the year, the First Lady came to him with a picture printed in a copy of the *Ladies' Home Journal,* he once more lauded the man's great artistic talent with the camera. The picture he now looked at was that of a painting made from Curtis' prize-winning photograph of Marie Fischer, a Seattle child. The magazine had arranged with the well-known painter, Walter Russell, to paint twelve of the country's children judged most beautiful by the publication. The one Edward Curtis had taken had won first prize and was here reproduced.

"Edith," the President said, "there can be no question about it—and it's a bully idea. We must invite Mr. Curtis to Sagamore Hill to take pictures of the children. We'll do it. Oh, he'll agree, all right."

The invitation came in due time and Edward Curtis went to the President's country estate eagerly, considering it a high privilege and the most delightful of relaxations from the strenuous season in the field. He set up headquarters half a mile from Sagamore Hill and in the weeks that followed became a fast family friend. The dinner parties in the country and those at the White House, both attended by old friends from the Harriman Expedition and fellow members of the Cosmos Club, were the most sparkling events of his life. He found TR a man with a vast expanse of knowledge and an insatiable curiosity about every subject under discussion.

This friendly association with the President reached its highest point when Curtis was asked to be official photographer at the most celebrated wedding in the United States, when Alice Roosevelt became Mrs. Nicholas Longworth. It was a signal honor and Curtis accepted it graciously. No other cameras were allowed at the ceremony or at the reception at "Friendship," the country home of John R. McLean. Curtis always chuckled when he remembered how the newspaper and magazine representatives were compelled to use "Exclusively Curtis" photographs for all releases. But what he recalled most vividly was TR's hearty voice on the telephone.

"Curtis, we're going to have lunch pretty soon. Come on over and make us some of that roquefort dressing of yours."

CHAPTER SIX

Fortunes
in the Field

T HE Turtles," wrote Edward Curtis of one experience in the field, "were ultra-mysterious objects. I had learned there were two of them in charge of a Keeper named Packs Wolf. The Mandans asserted that no white man had ever touched or had more than a possible glimpse of them. Naturally this intrigued me. I was most anxious to see them and photograph them.

"Our camp was miles away in the Arikara region of North Dakota, so I sent an interpreter, Upshaw, to do some scouting. Nothing beats an Indian in meeting Indian argument. He was gone almost two months and then came to me one beautiful frosty morning right at dawn to report that Packs Wolf was weakening in his protective resolve but that in order to see the Turtles it would be necessary to wait until early winter and then go secretly to him. Packs Wolf lived away from the main tribe and kept the Turtles in a detached log house.

"The snow was deep when we arrived, Upshaw and I. The temperature was sub-zero and the wind swept down across the bluffs seemingly direct from the polar regions. We were expected. Packs Wolf had with him two medicine men, confederates in this unethical affair. We warmed our chilled bodies in his tent and began to talk in a roundabout way of what we had come for. It was made very clear to me this business was being done without permission from the tribe and if we went ahead with it, a party of men might come and break up the proceedings. Dire things could happen to all of us.

"Packs Wolf explained that before going into the House of the Turtles it would be necessary to go through the purifying sweat, to make my body pure and acceptable to the Spirit People and the Turtles. I assured him I was quite willing to do this and we prepared for it. The sweat lodge, a small dome-shaped frame of willow saplings with a covering of blankets, was some distance from the house and near the edge of a cliff. Close by was the fire for heating the rocks. It was then well into the night and as I disrobed in a snowbank with the temperature twenty below and the wind blowing a gale, my enthusiasm cooled fast.

"Upshaw, the three Mandans and myself, took places sitting on our haunches with our backs to the blanket wall. Before us at our feet was a shallow pit and into this the attendant placed several hot rocks. Then the blanket opening was tightly closed and the singing began. At frequent pauses in the chant, water was poured on the rocks and one instantly forgot the outside temperature.

"Upshaw had warned me the Indians would impose a severe test, saying: 'If the heat becomes too great, lower your head to the ground and if necessary, raise an edge of the blanket to get a breath of cool air but don't do that unless you must, for it is not good form.' I did not explain to him I had been through many sweat lodges and had found that my Indian companions invariably had the same idea of a joke on the white man.

"However, it was an ordeal and I will not minimize it. The sweating was of four intervals of four songs each. At the end of the four songs, the blanket covering was raised slightly to give reviving fresh air, then a new supply of hot boulders was placed in the pit and then another series of four songs rendered. The fourth and final series was made the supreme test of endurance and the boiling so thorough I almost enjoyed the polar breezes while dressing.

"The following morning was the crucial hour. Would I see the Turtles or would some unforeseen happening upset all our plans? We at least were fortunate in the day. It was a real Dakota blizzard with little chance of suspicious Mandan braves snooping about.

"The House of the Turtles was of heavy logs, the door barred and windows covered. On entering we saw in the center of the room a large table, four by twelve feet. On it was piled a heterogeneous stack of offerings to the sacred objects—strips of calico and flannel, fetishes, skins, pipes, eagle feathers, plants, bead pouches containing umbilical cords, scalps, etc. The Keeper in a low voice rendered a short prayer to the Turtles, begging that they be not offended. He next removed the mass of offerings—and there was what I had gone to such lengths to see.

"The Turtle effigies were made of heavy buffalo hide, the pieces sewn together with rawhide. Each was about twenty inches across and later I g u e s s e d weighed about twenty pounds. Around the neck of each was an eagle-feathered necklace. I quickly made a picture of them, then asked if the feathers might be removed. The request occasioned considerable discussion between t h e Keeper and his helper; fear was expressed that the Turtles would be offended. In the end the Keeper delivered a lengthy prayer asking their permission, explaining this was at the request of a white man w h o had no understanding of sacred matters or the modesty of turtles. T h e feathers were removed with great care and reverence, the priest talking continually as though consoling children.

"With the sound of impending hoof beats almost in my ear, half expecting angry riders to appear any time, I made two exposures of the naked Turtles. Then I composed myself and asked the priest if I might move them slightly into a better light. To my surprise he acquiesed but warned against turning them over, saying 'for if you do we will all die.' I am certain no more tender touch was ever made than mine on those Turtles. I moved them, exposed t w o more plates and nodded. The priest quickly replaced the feather necklaces and recovered the Turtles with the mass of votive offerings, all the while begging their continued beneficence. Then he turned to me. 'Never before has a white man touched or been close to the Turtles.'"

"I felt myself suddenly drained of energy and reeking with perspiration, shaking like an aspen leaf. The fear of interruption before the pictures could be made had been nerve wracking. We had actually just finished packing and loading our saddle bags when the expected sight came. Over a slight rise in the snow-covered prairie came a band of twenty-five or more scouts and braves. With their horses snorting clouds of vapor in our group, the questioning Mandans found me making notes in a little book. I blew on my hands and told Upshaw to tell them we were learning about a tribal myth.

Florence Curtis with Yurok Guides—Klamath River, 1923

As we rode away I hoped we had convinced the riders our own story was not one too. Fortunately, taking a picture leaves no mark."

Every day and week researcher Curtis spent with exhibitions or on lecture tours, was the dross that came with the gold. It was the field work to which he turned with all the eagerness of a primitive, once society released him from the required task of getting money enough for the work. This was a problem even after he received the Morgan grant, for like many blessings, that had turned out to be mixed with difficulties.

"Immediately following the arrangement with Morgan and Company," he stated in one of his official reports, "plans were made for a vigorous field campaign and in April we were at work in the Apache country. During the spring, summer, autumn and the first half of the winter, we worked with the Apache, Navaho, Jicarilla Apache, Hopi, Pima, Papago, Havasupai, Qahatika, Yuma and Mohave. The season had its problems and obstacles but the results—tremendous. Our object was to complete the research for the first two volumes and every member of our party worked to the limit of his physical strength to that end. At the close of the field work our main party of three men and a stenographer settled down in obscure rooms to do the final work of getting those two volumes ready for publication. This consumed about ninety days and during all that time we all slept and took our meals at the rooms, in order to have no interruptions. I seldom went home to Seattle and not even my own family knew our whereabouts. Our regular working hours during those months were from eight in the morning until one the next morning, seven days a week. The day the manuscript was completed, Mr. Phillips took the material and went to Boston, to remain there and look after publication.

"In the meantime plans had been completed for another big year in the field, with a party larger than the previous one. We first worked with the many tribes of the Sioux, then the Mandan, the Arikara, the Hidatsa, Crow and Atsina, a year of great activity and splendid results. We closed the moving camp only when severe winter drove us from the field. Then another session of uninterrupted writing in a small log cabin in the mountains of Montana. There we settled down and took up work on Volumes III and IV.

"Our party consisted of four men. Breakfast hour was 7:30, beginning active work at 8:00; a half hour for lunch, an hour for supper, then working until 1:00 a.m. This was done every day of the month until spring. I did not take a day off during that time, the only interruption being a single trip to the post office, six miles away. I permitted mail to come to our camp but once a week and no newspapers were allowed. Every thought and every moment had to be given to the work. With the coming of spring, the manuscript was complete and ready for publication; but the financial panic was on and the world without money. The Seattle banks had agreed to make the necessary loans to publish these two volumes but now could not keep the promise. Notwithstanding the panic and lack of money, our subscribers would expect us to keep our contracts and publish the books.

"I went to New York and took up the fight for money. Just how I pulled through I do not know—largely by getting some of the more wealthy subscribers to pay their obligations in full; but it all meant four months of hard work in New York. Fortunately I had our regular field money and our party, headed by W. E. Myers and Edmond Schwinke, was at work. I joined them as soon as I could get away from New York.

"Our work that year was with the Arikara, Mandan, Cheyenne, Atsina, Yakima, Klickitat, Umatilla and Chinookan. In the early winter three of us hibernated in an isolated cabin on Puget Sound. Here we did the final work on Volumes V, VI and some on VII—several months of incessant work of fifteen hours a day, again with but one mail a week and no newspapers. Mr. Myers and I took two Sundays a month off and visited our families; and during the winter we had but one visitor and he but for a few minutes. The long strain of work here was such that I was seriously worn out toward the end and on the last week of the final reading and correcting of the manuscript, I could not leave my bed.

"The day work was finished on these volumes we broke our permanent camp and within a week were starting another field season, with the Nez Perce, then Kalispel, Piegan, Kutenai, Flathead. The following year the work was done largely by boat; first a trip down the Columbia River, then along the Washington coast and in British Columbia—a season of hard effort with good results. I had to handle my own boat, do my own work in regular picture making, collecting, and before the end of the season money was so scarce, I could not afford a cook, so I did that work myself."

In setting about the regular research work, Curtis had a general outline to follow, the twenty-five "cardinal points," as he called them, of a tribe's manners, customs, beliefs, etc. The outline was only theoretical and information was obtained as he could obtain it. In general, Curtis wanted to know:

1. Vocabulary
2. Primitive foods: methods of obtaining and preparing
3. Houses: dwelling, ceremonial, sudatory, menstrual, storage
4. Arts and industries: basketry, pottery, vessels and utensils for house and field, methods of land and water transportation, ornamentation, writing, agriculture, hunting, fishing
5. Games and pastimes
6. Measures and values
7. Dress of male and female: adornment with objects, by painting and tattooing, hair dressing of both sexes
8. Marriage customs: divorce, treatment of adulterers, prostitution, deviates
9. Naming and training of children
10. Maturity ceremony: customs attending attainment of puberty by both sexes
11. Mortuary customs: disposition of deceased personal property, mourning, purification after handling dead, taboo on names
12. Future world
13. Astronomical beliefs: conception of universe and natural phenomena
14. Political organization: manner of succession to chiefship—its duties and privileges; council, its powers, how assembled and who admitted; relation of bands composing tribe, or of tribes forming a confederacy; influence of shamans on politics and government
15. Social organization and customs: society, secret or military, or for purely social purposes; clans, their names and governing laws, restrictions and privileges, myths and legends; descent—paternal or maternal; property rights of husband and wife, rules of inheritance; intimacy or restriction of intimacy between those of various degrees of relationship, as between son-in-law

43

and mother-in-law; salutations and farewells

16. Earliest known habitat: legendary habitat; migrations, extent of territory dominated at various periods
17. Traditional enemies and allies: commercial relations
18. War customs: manner of organizing a party, duties of scouts and leaders, system of counting honors, methods of fighting, accounts of wars
19. Origin or creation myth
20. History: trace tribal history as far back as possible by whatever means, as by the lives of successive head chiefs, record of such material as can be had from local white residents, mentioning name of informant
21. Culture hero or transformer. Unless there is one definitely limited cycle of tales describing his exploits, collect a reasonable number of representative specimens, preferably such as are fit to publish
22. Other myths and folks tales
23. Medicine men: source of their power, manner of exercising it, description of healing ceremony if such exists; fraternity of shamans, their influence
24. Ceremonials in such detail as their relative importance warrants, noting especially the purpose, time and length of celebration, music and words of songs
25. Religion: a definite formulation of their conceptions, recording names of deities, functions, methods of worship and sacrifice, beliefs concerning t h e human spirit

Yet to have a plan in this work only meant there were great difficulties in following it, many of them insurmountable. There was always the hostile or reticent reception, the sudden caprice or unfounded suspicion. Some emergency might arise in the tribal councils, the camp might be forced to move. The weather or any of a dozen unpredictable causes might delay or lengthen the task and Curtis would be forced to leave the area and complete the research at a later date.

"For a general period of twenty years," he w a s always quick to reiterate, "I had the invaluable services of Mr. W. E. Myers. He was a rapid shorthand writer, a speedy typist who had majored in English literature and had developed an uncanny ear for phonetics. In spelling he was a second Webster.

"To the Indians his skill in phonetics was awesome magic. An old informant would pronounce a seven syllable word and Myers would repeat it without a second's hesitation, which to the old Indian was awe-inspiring—as it was to me. At most times while extracting information, Myers sat on my l e f t and the interpreter on my right. I led in asking questions, Myers and the interpreter prompted me if I overlooked any important points. What chance did the poor old Indian have when confronted by such a combination? By writing all information in shorthand we speeded the work to the utmost. Our trio could do more work in a year than a lone investigator, writing i n longhand, and lacking phonetic skill, could do in five years. That is why we did so much in the time we had. Also we knew nothing of labor unions in our party. Myers neatly typed his day's collection before going to bed. In that way field notes were kept up to the minute. Our average working time for a six months' season would exceed sixteen hours a day.

"By all odds the deepest wall to penetrate was that of the Indians' religion, their spiritual convictions and deep-rooted prejudices. I had q u i t e a time getting the

44

Apache creation myth. Preparatory to going into the field that year, I told an ethnological investigator in Washington I hoped to get Apache religious material. This was met with derision. 'You are going out to get something that doesn't exist. The Apaches have no religion.'

"Somewhat aghast at such a statement coming from a trained worker, I meekly asked on what basis he made that statement and told him I was under the impression that it was assumed by all students of man's development, that there could be no such thing as humans possessing speech and not possessing some form of religious belief. This also was derided. Having already learned considerable of the Apaches, I asked—'How do you know they have no religion?' 'I lived among them,' he said. 'I asked them and they told me they had no religion. And none of our workers could secure a word that they had religious beliefs of any sort.'

"Arriving at the reservation, the Apaches I had known beamed with delight, but when it was discovered I had returned with desire to learn something of their life, there was a sudden change in the atmosphere. Old friends looked the other way when passing. One of my former interpreters, learning of my purpose, declined to have anything to do with me—declaring he was not going out in search of sudden death. Another, a man possessing considerable knowledge, remained as steadfast as an Indian could be expected to, but he assured me that beyond the vaguest outline which he could personally give me, it would be impossible to secure information as to their beliefs. Subtlety and attempted bribery availed us nothing. At the end of six weeks of patient work we had only succeeded in building up a wall of tribal reticence. Every member of the tribe understood that no one was to talk with us and a delegation of the so-called chiefs had visited the agent in charge and demanded that I leave the reservation. The agent could only tell them that my authority for being there was direct from Washington and beyond his control unless I committed some overt act.

"With the greatest stealth I had approached several of the medicine men in an effort to secure even a key to the situation, my theory being that if I could secure a few words of information, I could use them as leverage in building up. But on the subject of religion these medicine men were as silent as the Sphinx.

"On the whole reservation there were not to exceed a dozen medicine men capable of giving a comprehensive outline of their mythology, and at the time of my visit there, there was great discord among these men. Das-lan, an ambitious medicine man, was promulgating a new cult. This he claimed had been revealed to him by the gods and through its furtherance, the canny old man hoped to supplant old Gosh-o-nne as head medicine man. This discord and strife among the wise men gave me my only hope. I was of the opinion that the fight might grow so bitter that some one of the priests would talk to us for retaliation for wrongs done him and as far as I have been able to learn, that was what occurred.

"Despite his several refusals, Gosh-o-nne seemed the most kindly disposed and we felt that he was our one hope. His camp was an isolated one, and by walking at night over a questionable trail, it was possible to visit him with small chance of observation.

"The summer was passing and we felt that we must accomplish something or give up in despair and go on to other tribes. So we decided to make a final effort to get Gosh-o-nne to talk. We were encouraged in this by our interpreter who told us the old man was so mad at the Das-lan group that he might talk.

"We reached the Gosh-o-nne camp at dawn. Concealed in a copse, we watched the old man emerge for his morning prayer to the sun. Then we approached and once more made our plea that he tell us how the world began. Without protest or comment, he stated: 'I think I will tell you that story.' Then he led us to a secluded spot among the shrubery at the brookside. First he invoked the sun in a short prayer, then without prelude he began the story of the gods and the creation of the earth and its people. It was midday before he reached the end and the explanations of functions of the characters involved. That is how we secured the Apache creation myth. In poetry of imagination I believe it is supreme in genetic legends collected from the American Indians.

"Months of trying, patient work were spent on the confirmation and amplification of the legend. But we never had opportunity to exchange further words with Gosh-o-nne. For the day after he talked with us, he sent for our interpreter and unburdened his soul. 'I am very sorry I talked,' he said. 'Spies watched and know that my words have gone to the white man. My words are on the white man's paper and I cannot take them back. Never before has an Apache told a white man those things which are our own. My life will be short; all the medicine men have said it. Tell those men I am sorry that I talked but I am not angry with them. They must not try to talk to me again. If they meet me on the trail, I am a stranger to them. They must not speak to me. That is what I ask.' We respected his request.

"Personal jealousies and ambitions of men within the tribes also got in m y way many times—and when an Indian wants to keep a secret, he will beat a Chinaman anytime. I developed a sixth sense that helped me greatly. I recall I wanted to photograph the 'cacique' or chief of a secret brotherhood and supreme ruler of a Tiwa village in New Mexico. The very existence of this brotherhood was held a dark secret.

"Even before I got to the village a runner approached me to say I could not camp near this place. I made this young man a present of a $5 bill and we rode on, meeting some more Tiwas. More presents, and finally permission to stay at the edge of the village—one day only. I stayed two days, studying every movement of every male person, finally concluding a certain dignified old Indian could very well be the cacique I was looking for.

"The chief came to tell me to leave and he wasn't very gentle about it, a crew following in case I gave any trouble. I frowned at him and pointed, and then walked where my finger pointed, to the house of the old Indian, where I p r o m p t l y sat tight on his doorstep. I engaged him in light conversation, talking about everything but the fact that I knew of the secret brotherhood and that I thought he was the cacique—all the time keeping my eye on the chief who did seem to be in some kind of quandary.

"He approached me again and said to go. 'No,' I told him. 'I can't go today.' I gestured toward my new-old friend. 'He is having his picture taken in the morning.' If the old man wondered about this he did not indicate it and the chief went away, as much as saying he had done all he could do and the matter was now out of his hands. This was a sound giveaway that my hunch had been right.

"I worked patiently with that slow-thinking old patriarch, urging him toward the photograph and the subject of that secret organization. His vanity and cupidity finally got the better of him. I took the picture in the bright light of morning and learned enough to assure me he was the cacique and as his friend, the chief would never use any authority on me."

46

CHAPTER SEVEN

The Vanishing Race Pauses

AT the beginning of his work on the North American Indian, Edward Curtis estimated it would take him fifteen years to cover all the tribes, some eighty of them. It took him thirty years. He had thought it might require the taking of perhaps ten thousand photographs. For the complete work he took over forty thousand. He had few detractors and even these agreed Curtis had accomplished a Herculean feat.

During the thirty years of his intense research and writing, his lectures and presence at exhibitions, the demands and pressures of the work left no time for any divertissement. He felt the need for refreshment and refurbishing of his spirit but he considered every temptation to "get away from it all" as something like an evil influence. Perhaps his most bitter disappointment, in terms of self-sacrifice, was his decision not to accompany Theodore Roosevelt as photographer on an African safari. Teddy's invitation was sincere and pressing, at the same time acknowledging the photo-historian's dedication to "his Indians." Curtis explained his professional reasons for declining the offer, assured that his friend understood them.

The pattern of his life had now changed. He spent little time in Seattle, almost all of it with the Indians or with his field crews preparing manuscripts for the book publication or in the eastern cities looking after money matters and fulfilling speaking engagements. It seemed advisable for his daughter, Beth, instead of going to college, to take charge of the Seattle studio in the Downs Building and then the new location at Fourth and University. She was very close to her father a n d his interests, had inherited his drive and tireless energy. In the studio she had the skillful help of a family friend, Ella McBride.

In 1913 came the sudden death of J. Pierpont Morgan and apprehension that the book publishing program might be canceled. Edward Curtis was in New York at this time and set to work at once on a financial report and account of the project, delivering it to auditors at the Morgan bank. After some anxious days, he received a telephone call from the bank with the information that Mr. Morgan's son wished to speak to him.

Curtis recalled vividly he was almost numb with worry when he went to keep the appointment. He had learned the elder Morgan's explorations in foreign countries had been closed by cable order, that all commitments for purchases of art objects and paintings had been nullified and that a great part of his art collection was being sold. He could see little hope for the North American Indian project being continued.

Young Morgan's greeting was cordial and his hand clasp firm. Without preliminaries he came directly to the point, and with every word Edward Curtis' tenseness eased.

"Mr. Curtis," Morgan said simply. "I can well understand your anxiety as to what is to be done about the North American Indian books. As a family we have discussed the matter thoroughly and have decided to finish the undertaking as father had in mind. We know that is what he would want us to do." He then outlined the plans he had in mind. All sales efforts would be discontinued, all energy a n d money directed toward the completion of field work and publication. The sales office on Fifth Avenue would be closed and all business matters handled from the Morgan bank.

With this crisis past and with grateful relief, Curtis attended a meeting of the North American Indian committee and impressed the group with a scholarly yet warm-hearted address as a tribute to his late friend and sponsor. This "Word of Appreciation of Mr. John Pierpont Morgan" was widely reprinted and editorialized.

"Since we last met the world has suffered a great loss. Owing to our association w i t h the one whose death is so profoundly felt throughout the land, this loss comes home to us as a personal one. The part of human effort which brings us together is directly a record of one of the races, and indirectly a study of man, his origin, his destiny.

For a time we put this aside and stand bowed before life's greatest mystery—death. How can a personality yesterday so vital—so powerful, today be still? Perhaps this means no lessening of human power. Perhaps such achievement is the inspiration which leads our evolution. Through ages beyond reckoning the human r a c e has steadily developed; has climbed like a towering shaft toward its ultimate destiny. Through these numberless ages, epoch after epoch has had its great men, each a part of and a forward step of the human race. It has been our good fortune to be associated with one whose mental endowment placed him thus at the fore-front of human development, whose talents were an achievement of the race, and one who so used those talents that he could rightly be called the foremost citizen of the t i m e. To accomplish this i s an achievement indeed.

Mr. Morgan in his exceptional generosity has done many great services to the world of art and literature, but I believe that the verdict of future generations will be that one of his greatest gifts to humanity is this record of the American Indian. The native of North America has given Science its best opportunity to study man at a most interesting period geologically speaking, the period immediately following the acquisition of implements, the period when he was yet awkward in the use of such tools as his sluggishly inventive brain had evolved and before the inventive faculty h a d yet fully awakened to the fact that successful existence depended upon reason rather than instinct. Viewed in this way we have a more comprehensive idea as to the value of this work to the world of learning. The study of the Coptic manuscripts is of the greatest value in biblical study. This research dealing with the primitive American which his help has furthered, will be of the utmost value in the study of man and his development. It is a source of great regret to me that Mr. Morgan could not have lived to see his task completed, but as that was not to be, my greatest desire now is to conduct and complete the w o r k in a way which will justify his cooperation.

I beg that these words may be considered with the records of the North American Indian and further that a copy may be sent to the family of Mr. Morgan.

Edward S. Curtis

Returning then to the West Coast, he devoted more time to his independent writing. He had been preparing a book f o r children—*Indian Days of Long Ago*—and in 1 9 1 5 it was accepted for publication by the World Book Company of New York, to be issued as part of its series, *Indian Life and Indian Lore*. Encouraged by this acceptance, the author set to work on a second book—*Land of the Headhunters*. This too was welcomed by the publishers and brought out later that same year. Sales of the b o o k s eventually reached over two million copies.

In 1914 he wrote a motion picture script b a s e d on his experiences in getting material for the second volume and produced the picture on the Fort Rupert Indian Reservation in the Kwakiutl area of British Columbia. Curtis directed all the action through his native interpreter. The photoplay, *L a n d   o f   t h e   Head   H u n t e r s*, was launched with the help of an experienced producer and enjoyed considerable success.

He was now able to devote more time to the Curtis Picture Musicales. For several years these were a form of cultural entertainment popular in the larger cities a n d supplied an important contribution to the field work fund. The presentations were handled by a New York booking agent whose method was primarily to secure the sponsorship of clubs or women's societies. Edward Curtis was paid on a percentage of attendance basis.

The musicales were billed under the heading, "The Story of A Vanishing R a c e" and either of two lectures given, on the Southwestern or Northwestern Indians. They were advertised as "Entertainment of Educational Value," and were composed of lecture, colored stereoptican slides and motion pictures usually accompained by Indian music played by an orchestra of nine pieces.

In the latter days of the Indian investigations, when the field studies had been refined with an adequate staff, Curtis had made recordings of the tribal music and songs, using an early day diamond-needle phonograph and wax cylinders. For the lectures these were turned over to Henry F. Gilbert of Boston as themes and inspiration for more formal musical compositions.

It was now easier to get cooperation from the Indians and this added more to the book information, gave Curtis better pictures and more enthusiasm for other phases of the work, such as the lectures and musicales. At almost every Indian camp he was now greeted with marked friendliness and even eagerness. The Indians felt they could n o w trust him and were not only willing but anxious to help. They had begun to grasp the idea that his work was to be a permanent memorial to their race and it appealed to their imagination. They did not want to be left out.

"Tribes that I won't reach for four or five years," he once mentioned at a lecture, "have sent me word to come and see them. If they haven't hit upon the idea themselves, I suggest to them—'Such and such a tribe will be in this record and you won't. Y o u r children will try to find you in it and won't be able to and they will think you didn't amount to anything at all, while the other tribe will be thought to be big people.'"

"Is there any one formula for making the Indian talk?" he was asked.

"The key to penetrating the Indian's reserve and making him talk confidentially is to get into his religious and devotional life. Before you can get him to talk on such subjects you must reach a point where you can discuss his religion with him on even terms— not merely ask questions about it. That is a most difficult point to get at. With most investigators it is the last thing to take up. I made it the first.

"I couldn't make pictures of their religious ceremonies unless I entered into their inner life and understood it from their standpoint. That means I have to make a study of comparative religions and when I meet Indians I must be able to bring them a basis for discussion. It isn't merely a matter of going through one tribe and coming away full of information about it. I began my work among the Pueblos thirteen years ago and haven't yet published the volume that is to deal with them. I go to them, study some village, go away and return to study another.

"The Pueblos have a tremendous devotional or rather ceremonial life and they a r e secretive about it above most Indians. It is an aggregation of secret orders a n d one order will have no knowledge of what occurs in another fraternity. So after you have a thorough knowledge of one group you are still far away from complete insight into their life.

"Snake worship, it is true, runs through all the groups b u t with each it varies greatly. The Hopi Snake Ceremony is also intensely dramatic. After m y third visit to one Hopi group, I was invited to take part as a priest. I am a priest in other nations too but I am especially proud of my participation in the Hopi ceremony. If I went back to Arizona today I could officiate in the snake dance—in the order to which I belong.

"Then you were adopted into the tribe?"

"No, that isn't necessary. Being adopted into a tribe is nothing. The thing i s to become a member of a secret order. That is the only way to learn their secrets. And every ceremonial group you get into makes it easier to get into others. Belonging to the Snake Order in one village wouldn't necessarily let me into an order in another village but it would give me good ground to make an argument.

"As I recall it was twelve years between my first season with the Hopis and the year when I participated in the Snake Dance at the village of Walpi. During that time I spent part of four seasons at different Hopi villages a n d worked with fourteen Indian informants.

"When first seeing that sacred dance, I was determined to build up a friendship with the Snake Priest and work toward participation in t h e ceremony. I succeeded so well in this, that twelve years later I took part in the whole of it, from the gathering of the snakes until they were released in the desert.

"I fasted with the Hopis, wore the costume of a priest, painted my body in t h e sacred manner and slept in the kiva beside a native priest who was my informant and interpreter. Since I was a novitiate, the snakes were placed around m y neck before going into the bags. I complied with all the rules and requirements, including no contact w i t h others of my party and complete celibacy."

On some of his field expeditions Curtis was accompanied by Edmond S. Meany, professor of history at the University of Washington, an Indian authority and Curtis enthusiast. He recalled many experiences on the trail.

"I have met and worked with many ethnologists, archaeologists, linguists, historians, artists and none came so close to the Indian as Curtis did. He actually seemed part of their life. I heard a rugged old chief ask him once—'How d i d you learn to be just like Indian?' He would discuss religious topics in a circle of tribesmen as they passed the pipe and they would say—'He is like us. He knows about the Great Mystery.' It was masterful the way he could handle those Indians, friendly or hostile.

"I went on one trip with him into the South D a k o t a Bad Lands. BA-ZAHOLA WASH-TI—that was what the Sioux called him. We had as guide Chief Red Hawk a n d one morning Curtis told him to set up a camp on the banks of the Wounded Knee for himself and his twenty followers while we two white men went up the river a piece to get some photographs. Curtis promised a feast when we returned at night.

Curtis and daughter Beth in Eskimo Kaiak

"When we got back we found, instead of twenty, a camp of at least three hundred, including several chiefs of Red Hawk's rank. He told us he could not control the invitations and all these people had decided to stay. Chief Slow Bull had brought his council tipi which was decorated with buffalo hides, a horse's tail floating from the peak.

"Curtis had no intention of feeding all those people even if he h a d had the beef, so he called for a council and made a speech, saying Chief Red Hawk h a d twenty men and they were now going to eat, Curtis and I with them. Chief Iron Crow spoke up. He needed more beeves than Ba-zahola Wash-ti had provided. Yes. Yes. Everybody said they needed beeves too and there were many 'hows' and handshakes. Then Chief Slow Bull raised his hand majestically and quieted the restless mob. He said he too needed more beeves. Then all seemed to quiet down and Curtis said they would probably all go home. But then consternation struck when one Indian, in trying to load a s u g a r bag of oats, dropped it. Everything was out of control again, all the hungry Indians excited to what seemed to me the danger point.

"Mind you, Curtis had traveled many weary miles for the pictures he hoped to get with Red Hawk and his men. Yet now he resolutely folded his camera and started to pack up. He did not grumble, showed no impatience, offered n o recriminations. As he packed he discussed things in general with the chiefs and then we moved off, leaving Red Hawk and his twenty men with the others, while we made our camp up river.

"In the morning, everything had changed. Here came Red Hawk and Slow Bull leading all their warriors. Everybody was happy and wanted to help the white friend get pictures. Old rites were reenacted. Old battles fought again, old stories retold—all recorded in the Curtis camera and fastened on the mind that knew s o well how to handle Indians."

51

Expedition Boat "Jewel Guard" at King Island, Alaska

The last trip for material was the long one to the Arctic in 1927 when the Curtis party secured rare pictures and data on whale hunting, seal herds, the natives of Nunivak, King Island, Little Diomede, Cape Prince of Wales and Kotzebue—all this for the twentieth and last volume of books. It was a rigorous trip, most of it covered in a forty-foot boat, and almost made disastrous by the Arctic storms. Beth Curtis made the voyage with her father and party, by steamer *Victoria* to Nome.

The landing here on June 20 carried Edward S. Curtis back twenty-n i n e years to the time he had seen Nome as the gold-mad mining settlement, little more than a cluster of tents, the beach black with feverish miners. It was different now. The floors and walls of the hotel sagged in all directions, only a few windows with glass in them. H a l f the buildings were vacant, others decaying. It was a town which had lived in a high, wide and handsome way and now was dying.

It is very probable these sad evidences had more effect on the man Curtis than he showed or admitted. He was fifty-nine years old, his business interests no longer in Seattle but centered in the Curtis Studio in Los Angeles which h e operated with his daughter Beth. In southern California also were his son Harold and daughter Katherine, Mrs. Ray Ingram, affectionately known as Billy.

And he was engaged in making the last volume of t h e *North American Indian*, writing under severe handicaps. The creative load itself was crushing and only with Beth's devotion, moral support and hard work was he able to complete the final book. It is to be supposed he knew he had made his last reach into the Indian treasure house.

CHAPTER EIGHT

Rewards of Accomplishment

MY father was a man with great singleness of purpose," his daughter Florence has said. "When he was working on any phase of his photography career, he was never to be dissuaded from his main objective. At home in Seattle he was either searching for data, getting equipment and material ready for a field trip, or improving on his processes of photography and printing. And when we thought he might be coming home, he was in New York getting money or looking after the details of the book publishing. We always said he had no home life at all.

"All this meant, of course, great sacrifice of the things most people need to lead a satisfying life—participating in sports, recreation, gardening and other avocations, but father didn't seem to need those safety valves. He was big, six feet two inches, husky, ruggedly built yet with this he had a soft voice with a pleasing tone to it that inspired confidence.

"He was a driver, especially as far as Edward Curtis was concerned, yet never with money in mind except what he needed to carry on the work. At the time we didn't think of him as a genius but later, with proper perspective, we knew he was. Like most great men he seemed to have little sense of personal gain. Everything he did was directed toward the main theme of preparing material for the *North American Indian* and other writings about the tribes. His life was certainly dedicated to an ideal.

"It is well known that father had remarkable rapport with the Indians yet he never attempted to impose his own ideas on them—the ideal type of reporter. I remember one trip I made with him up the Klamath River in Northern California, in the country of the Yuroks and Karoks. An Indian girl came to our camp one night saying her grandmother was very sick and could the white man help.

"We followed her to where the old woman was lying on a cot. I thought father would try to get a doctor. That seemed to be what the girl wanted, being of the younger generation. But father said—'That woman needs an Indian doctor,' and told the girl to get the tribe's medicine man. He came in full regalia and we left. The next night the grandmother was reported in better condition and father told me that was the way it should be, that the Indian had faith in tribal medicine and faith was what cured their sick.

"And besides his persuasive manner, father had another trait which helped him get information from both natives and white people. He was an excellent conversationalist with a great fund of information on birds, trees and animals. He loved nature in all its forms and naturally absorbed many facts about it.

"He had many ideas too about the treatment of the Indians and while he spoke of it only occasionally, and then not with any vehemence or rancor, he kept this attitude out of his books. He did bring it out in some of his magazine articles, however. For the old *Hampton's* Magazine he was interviewed by Edward Marshall and one of the questions was—'What might we Americans have made of the Indians?' This is part of father's answer:

" 'The Indians could have given us that physical vigor which must be one of the foundations of any lasting and important mental strength; they could have helped us in the creation of a literature, for they were marvelous in the b e a u t y of their free, poetic thought, full of imagery such as white men have never known—their souls were those of poets. They could have helped us in our music, for theirs was a real part of their lives, a genuine expression of emotion. They could have aided us vastly in our decorative art. And in a broad sense, they could have helped us in our morals, for in all their dealings they were fair until we taught them theft and lying.

" 'Their lives were often ruled by high impulses, sometimes rising to real grandeur of self-sacrifice in their consideration for their fellows. They were untainted by commercialism. Their pride might well have been transmuted into a mighty asset for the new race we were forming, but we preferred to graft upon the sturdy stock of independence, which induced our forefathers to cross the seas, the sad subservance of worn-out peoples, incapable of taking the great plunge of immigration until the way had been prepared for them and made comparatively easy, fleeing to us finally, only after they had been crushed into bent-backed humility and dull-eyed apprehension by centuries of violent oppression.'

"Mr. Marshall then asked him—'What did we make of him?'

" 'We have made of him,' father said, 'a race totally discouraged. We h a v e robbed him of the last thing, which through ages of association and race-building, he had learned to love. Think of it, the melancholy of it, for the Indian and for his conquerors! He knows well that, as he now is, after the century and more of wrong we have inflicted on him, he cannot adjust himself to the environment we press on him. He has been handled very maladroitly, and is perfectly aware of it, and is tortured by it. But forced to the wall, with no escape, he has accepted his dull fate with the grim stoicism of his race, and has ceased to try to combat or avert it. Our efforts to extend assistance to him have been insincere and he has known it; linked, unwillingly, with cupidity and stupid lack of understanding, even the work of those few honest men who really have tried to help him has been wasted—has been worse than wasted, for it has been harmful.'

" 'We have always wronged the Indian but the greatest wrongs we are doing him today are born of our misunderstanding of him. The hardest of his manifold misfortunes came through the ever-changing policies by which we managed him after he had been fully conquered. We have ever been and still are vacillating and uncertain in our dealings with him, just as instability of method in the conduct of its commerce would ruin any business corporation.' "

In her late years, Eva Curtis remembered her older brother as a serious-minded boy who matured early. He took responsibility easily and even in his teens possessed a professional manner. She recalls him as the breadwinner of the family after their father died and the bad year they all had when Edward fell off a log and hurt his leg. Yet he showed full courage and determination to get his pictures of Indians and still make enough of a living to keep the family going.

His daughter Beth also knew this physical courage well from their early days and later on the trips she made with him. They had mutual admiration and respect for each other as is shown by Edward Curtis' many references to Beth's help, in the Seattle studio and later in Los Angeles.

"I think that was father's greatest quality, courage coupled with great curiosity. I don't mean courage so much in the lack of fear because I think h e did feel fear and was strong enough to overcome it. I mean his ability to think positively instead of negatively —and that takes genuine courage sometimes. He always had his sights set high and didn't look below them, just kept pushing on toward that goal with his natural aggressiveness and strength of character.

"You couldn't defeat him if you tried. Nothing seemed to. Once in the Canyon de Chelly in Arizona, a flash flood took away his cameras and plates—hundreds of wonderful pictures. What did he do? He got other cameras and went back and took other pictures. He had trip after trip where hard luck would have discouraged some men. There was that time he was whaling with the Kwakiutl Indians and lost the movie film when a slap of the whale's tail smashed the canoe. He would have lost his life then too if he hadn't been such a g o o d swimmer. Indomitable—that's the word for my father.

"People are interested in the methods father used in taking his Indian pictures. Most of the field trips were made with horses and wagons, and in the more inaccessible areas with just horses. When he first started in earnest he used a 14x17 view camera— a big, cumbersome affair. Later he came down in size to 11x14 and finally to a 6x8 reflex camera. His most valuable possession was an old German l e n s he picked up in Seattle. He made all the head and shoulder shots in his tent which was lined w i t h maroon-colored material and had a skylight opening on one side with a curtain to control the light.

"Almost all the pictures were taken on glass plates w h i c h were heavy, hard to handle and easily broken which was always tragedy. The plates were packed in trunks, changed into the holders in a changing bag or in the tent at night. Each expedition into the Indian country required a tremendous amount of equipment and baggage. In addition to the photographic equipment and recording machine for the ceremonials and folk songs, he had to take tents, food and all personal things, sometimes for a party of four.

"Many times people have asked me what tribe father considered the finest, the highest type. I have never been able to answer that without qualifications. He spent m o r e time with the Apaches and Hopis and considered the Blackfeet and Nez Perces very intelligent people. I know he enjoyed working with the Kwakiutl and Haida s c a hunters. But he had great sympathy for the Sioux. In writing on the various Sioux tribes he said:

"In gathering the lore of the Indian today one hears only of yesterday. His thoughts are of the past; today is but a living death and his very being is permeated with the hopelessness of tomorrow. If the narrator is an ancient, nearing the end of his days, he lives and relives life when the tribe flourished as a tribe, the times when his people were truly monarchs of all they surveyed, when teeming buffalo supplied their every want; and his wish is ever that they might have passed away ere he knew the beggary of today. The younger man, if a true Indian, is a living regret he is not of the time when to be an Indian was to be a man.

"Perhaps among no tribe has the encroachment of civilization wrought greater change than among the Sioux or Dakota. Proud, aggressive people, they depended wholly on the chase and indigenous vegetation. Powerful in numbers, vigorous in sport, they roamed almost at will. But in a brief time, all was altered. The game had vanished. Under treaty stipulations which the Indians ill understood, they were concentrated on reservations beyond the borders of which they must not wander; and became dependents of the nation, to be fed and clothed according to our interpretation of compact.

"Of the present condition of the Sioux there is little that is encouraging. They have small hope of the future, and people without courage and hope are indeed a serious problem. In a few years will have passed away all who knew the old life. The younger generation, having no tribal past, may try to carve a future and their children, with even less instinct of the hunter, may make even better an advance; but standing in the way of the present generation, and all those to come, is the fact that they are Indians and lack by many ages that which is necessary to enable them to meet the competition of the Caucasian race.

No doubt thinking such thoughts as he reviewed his life, Edward S. Curtis died in Los Angeles on October 21, 1952, at the age of eighty-four. During his latter days he had acquired an interest in mining and in an expedition to South American mines, and in writing a book—*The Lure of Gold*. He had also worked as a "still" photographer in Cecil B. De Mille's film classic—*Ten Commandments*. Yet no one would deny the fact that Edward Curtis' life was bound into his prodigious *North American Indian* and when that work was published and accepted over the world, his own work was essentially done. It could be said these words from his introduction to the twenty volumes speak the story of his life with the Indians:

"The task has not been an easy one, for although lightened at times by the readiness of the Indians to impart their knowledge, it more often required days and weeks of patient endeavor before my assistants and I succeeded in overcoming the deep-rooted superstition, conservatism and secretiveness so characteristic of primitive people, who are ever loathe to afford a glimpse of their inner life to those who are not of their own. Once the confidence of the Indians was gained, the way led gradually through the difficulties, but long and serious study was necessary before knowledge of the esoteric rites and ceremonies could be gleaned.

"At the moment I am seated by a beautiful brook that bounds through the forests of Apacheland. Numberless birds are singing their songs of life and love. Within my reach lies a tree, felled only last night by a beaver, which even now darts out into the light, scans his surroundings and scampers back. A covey of mourning doves flies to the water's edge, the small birds slaking their thirst in a dainty way and fluttering off. By the brookside path now and then wander prattling children; a youth and a maiden hand in hand wend their way along the cool stream's brink. The words of the children and lovers are unknown to me but the story of childhood and love needs no interpreter.

"It is thus near to Nature that much of the life of the Indian still is; hence its story, rather than being replete with statistics of commercial conquests, is a record of the Indian's relations with and his dependence on the phenomena of the universe—the trees and shrubs, the sun and stars, the lightning and rain—for these to him are animate creatures. Even more than that, they are deified, therefore are revered and propitiated, since upon them man must depend for his well being."

Southwest Tribes

Apache - Jicarilla Apache - Navaho

. . . in the deserts and forested mountains of Arizona and New Mexico

At the Shrine—Navaho

Edward Curtis found many cairn shrines in various parts of Navaho reservation. As he happened by one, the tribesman gathered a few twigs of pinon or cedar, placed them on shrine, scattered a pinch of sacred meal over them, made supplication for what he habitually needed or for the demands of the moment.

Canyon de Chelly in Navaho Land

The Canyon de Chelly was one of the Navaho strongholds and Edward Curtis found evidence that it had been occupied by many other people in former times. High on every side cliff w e r e perched the ruins of villages belonging to many tribes and even races. The Navahos pictured as "The Vanishing Race" in frontispiece were entering the dark shadows of the defile leading to Canon de Chelly.

Hilltop Camp—Jacarilla Apache

The Navahos were second only to the Sioux in number, were the American Bedouins—plateau dwellers of the Southwest. They acknowledged no living superior, paid allegiance to no king or chief, were keepers of flocks and herds which they drove from the flat grass lands up the mountain sides and down again, according to seasons and weather. They asked nothing of the government except to be left alone in their pastoral surroundings, a desire refused.

The cunning Apaches gave long and fearless resistance to subjection by missionary and government. They were the scourge of peaceable Indians and for 300 years menaced the western colonists. When policies in Washington vacillated between simpering peace and full extermination, the Apaches retaliated with intermittent raids and flight into Mexico. The bounties set on the heads of men, women and children drove them deeper into savagery until subdued by General Crook.

Geronimo—Apache

Curtis found in this benign old man no sign of the infamous warrior, the scourge of the desert. He saw Geronimo in Washington, D. C. where the Apache had come to plead with The Great White Father, after knowing him in his native Arizona hills. Here he would gaze wistfully into the distance and speak of days when he had pride with complete inability to understand the guile and treachery of the white scouts and soldiers.

A Point of Interest—Navaho

Nesjaja Hatali—Navaho Medicine Man

Son of the Desert—Navaho

In the early morning, just after daybreak, this boy appeared at Curtis' camp. He approached like a tame squirrel, great curiosity shining in his eyes. He asked a dozen simple questions, striving to grasp the meaning of all things about him, the why and wherefore of nature and life itself.

The Renegade Type

The Lost Trail

Apache Babe

Jacarilla Matron

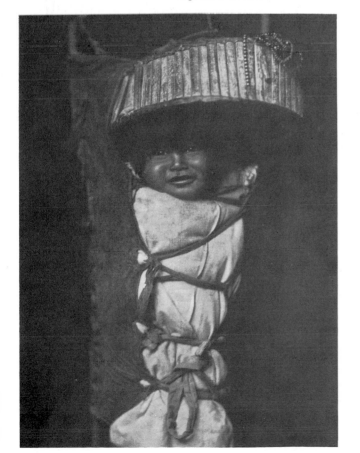

Mohave - Pima - Maricopa - Walapai

. . . in the mesquite, cottonwood and cactus of Arizona and eastern California

Pima Ki

The ki was the old-time round dwelling of the Piman tribes, in construction much like the earth lodge of the Northern plains Indians except top was almost flat, with no opening for escape of smoke and no extended entrance way. It was adequate shelter in the mild winter, smoke from small fire flowing out doorway and absorbed by earthen roof.

The Pima, in Arizona and extending into Sonora, Mexico, and eastern California, were from one point of view the ideal Indian, said Edward Curtis. They were industrious, keen of mind, tractable and friendly to civilization. They accepted the early Spanish missionaries but were never influenced deeply away from the religion of their ancestors, were Christians in name only. They lived by agriculture and the abundance of deer, birds and fish, had skill with handiwork to spin and weave cotton into blankets.

The Mohave life was barren of ceremony and ritualism. The tribe was a branch of the Yuman family living on the banks of the Colorado River in Arizona, earlier from Black Canyon to Needles. The men and women were big-boned, well-knitted, clear-skinned, yet mentally slow and dull—products of the hot, dry environment. They lived in rancherias wherever they could raise melons, corns, beans, squash and kill rabbits, rats, ducks and quail. Men wore simple breech cloths, women short skirts of willow bark softened in water and woven.

Mat Stams—Maricopa

Pachilawa—Walapai Chief

Judith—Mohave

The Maricopa were also Yuman, living generally on the banks of the Gila River in Arizona. Their living habits varied from the Pima in that they ate the fruit of the giant cactus—fresh, dried, made into jelly and wine. Like other Yuman tribes they burned their dead with ceremonies for important men. The Maricopa medicine men believed they had acquired through dreams the gift of healing disease.

The Yuman name Walapai meant "Pinery People." Curtis found but 500 in the tribe, living in the pine-clad mountains for about 100 miles along the south side of the Grand Canyon in Northwest Arizona. Wretched, poverty-stricken, with no native ground for agriculture, no stock for grazing, they earned meagre livings by hiring out to the railroads or any employer they could find. Dwellings were the rudest kind of shelters built of cedar boughs and brush. They raised a few scanty crops of corn and beans, killed jack rabbits and deer.

Mohave Water Carrier

Mother is shown on the bank of the Colorado River. Curtis found the Mohave women inclined to be large, very strongly built. They carried practically all burdens on their heads, could balance weighty loads a man would find all he could do to pick up, and still carry more in each hand.

Mosa—Mohave

Edward Curtis saw no more aboriginal type in his life with 80 Indian tribes than this Mohave girl. He said: "She had the eyes of a fawn as it emerges from the forest, questioning all the strange sights, sounds and colors of civilization. Such types Father Garus may have viewed on his journey through Mohave country in 1776."

Quiniaika—Mohave

Pima Woman

Resting in the Harvest Fields

Maricopa Girl

Hopi - Acoma

. . . dwellers on the desert mesas of Central Arizona

East Side of Walpi Village

In the dawn-yellow light of the eastern sky, the Hopi village crier urged men and women to their community and family duties. Burros were driven from stone corrals at mesa's edge, down winding trails, across the sands to the low-lying areas which caught freshet waters from table lands above. Here were the little fields of corn, beans, melons, squash, cultivated with hourly interruptions for prayers for rain.

People of peace through religious principles, the Hopi life was rich in mythology and ceremony. Edward Curtis visited seven cliff-perched villages in central Arizona-Walpi, Shongopovi, Shipaulovi, Mishongnovi, Sichomovi, and Oraibe. He found the people less s e c r e t i v e than many other tribesmen, living in obedience to the command of their god, Poseyamo or Creator, who counseled them to live in harmony with others until the stars told them of his coming. Then if they were to fight, he would lead.

Many times, as the historian worked with his camera or sought interviews with some Hopi patriarch, he would suddenly see a naked, bronze-skinned man of holy orders running from his kiva to a spring to deposit the pahos or prayer plume in the life-giving waters so the gods of North, East, South and West might see and send an answer.

Old Well of Acoma

The Acoma were the bravest of the Pueblo Indians, having fought the Spanish invaders with fierce resistance. Superficially a smiling, hospitable people, they were "fiends when angered," Curtis said, "like purring cats with sheathed but ever-ready claws." Devout followers of the Catholic Church, they obeyed only their primitive instincts, practiced only their native ceremonial rites.

Acoma Woman

Prayer to the Sun by Hopi Snake Priest

Appearance of Hopi Snake Dancers

At right stand the Antelopes, in front of snake jars. The Snakes enter plaza, encircle it four times with military tread, singing series of songs remarkable for creating irresistible movement, then dance with reptiles.

HOPI SNAKE DANCE

Although the Hopi Snake Dance itself consumed less than one half hour, as Edward Curtis described it, the important and most mystifying aspect was the preparation for the ritual. "It takes place during the full moon o f August when the Arizona mesas are powder dry and the Hopi's worst enemies are fire and crop failure, with the fear of famine. The Snake Dance symbolizes the desire for rain and a bountiful harvest, expressing itself in the worship of ancestors and origin of t h e race. The serpents depicted in paintings and on the walls represent lightning, the prayers offered by the medicine men directed toward the God of Clouds. The colors used in their decorations and ornaments are significant—yellow for pumpkins, green for corn and red for fruit.

"For eight days prior to the beginning of the ceremony, certain young men of the Hopi tribe are properly anointed b y the medicine men and sent out with bags to the four points of the compass to catch snakes of all kinds including rattlers. Each of them may account for any number from a hundred to five hundred. These are given to the care of skilled herders or charmers who guard them as sacred charges. T h e snakes have the complete freedom of the ceremonial house, Estufa, but their deadly fangs are rendered harmless as the reptiles are held in stupefaction, bemused by the action of the sacred eagle wands.

"In the hands of the guards, these wooden wands with their green handles on which snakes are pictured, eagle feathers tipping the ends, have a stultifying effect. When a snake grows restless and attempts to find liberty, the wand is gently brushed back and forth across its head, the snake cowering and becoming docile, allowing the guard to push it back with its fellows. The Hopis believe the snake has d r e a d of its enemy the eagle,

72

Acoma Belfry

whose habit is to brush the head with its wings to anger it. If the snake lunges, it strikes feathers only, and having expended its strength it lies exhausted and is easy prey to the eagle's talons. The action of the eagle wand simulates the eagle-wing motion of which the snake has learned to become wary.

"The dancers and painted priests form a long procession to the accompaniment of shrill drum beats, like the rattle of rain. They circle around the sacred rock, buffalo lodge and cottonwood tree in full leaf. Each dancer is naked except for a loin cloth ornamented with pictures of writhing serpents. The bare bodies are painted greenish black with broad white bands around the arms. Dangling in the rear are skins of f o x and coyote, around the neck are strings of shells with feathers on the crown of the head, long black hair in wild disarray about the face.

"The snakes are gripped in the teeth and held subdued by the gentle fanning of the eagle wands. From time to time, as the dance progresses, they are handled and tossed about by young boys who dart in among the dancers, sprinkling the sacred c o r n meal, imprisoning the snakes for a few minutes in the buffalo lodge where the priests pray over them within the sacred circle. The ocean appears as one figure in t h e ceremony which suggests that the ancestral home lay across some body of water.

"At the close of the dance, the thousands of snakes are caught up in great armfuls by the swift runners who race along the trails and down to the bases of precipices where they are released to the north, south, east and west where they were gathered. The entire ceremony is short but very vivid, making a striking impression upon the memory."

73

Counting the Record

Series of marks cut into the rock at Middle Mesa records losses inflicted on marauding enemies in a former generation.

Hopi Man

Here are the dominant traits of Hopi character, Edward Curtis noted. "The eyes are wary, perhaps with distrust, the mouth unyielding in stubbornness. Yet behind the mask are warmhearted friendliness and sense of humanity."

Hopi Snake Dancer in Costume

White markings typify the Antelope, indicate the man is dressed for the next-to-last day of Snake Dance when public performance consists of dance itself and ceremonial race of Antelope Fraternity.

The Potter—Numpeyo

Tiwa - Keres

. . . in the pueblos, forests and fields of New Mexico

Paguate Watchtower

Paguate was the oldest and largest of the ten villages subsidiary to Laguna, the parent pueblo of the group. Watchtower was erected as defense from roaming Navahos.

In religious beliefs and practices, Edward Curtis found the Pueblo Indians of the Rio Grande Valley the most conservative tribes in North America. This seemed to be due to the efforts of the early Franciscan missionaries to implant Christianity at the expense of the Indians' own deep-rooted beliefs which compelled them to practice their own rites in secrecy and in secluded places.

The villages of Santo Domingo, Acoma, Cochiti and Laguna represented the Keres linguistic family— Isleta and Taos, the Tiwa group of Tanoan stock. Coronado's force, wintering in the Tiwa villages in 1540-41, was the direct cause of nearly four centuries of Pueblo resistance.

76

Replastering Paguate House

Ah Pas—Taos on Antelope River

Jemez Fiscal

Fiscal was charged with supervision of church activities such as
burial of dead. Church was imposed on Pueblo life, was nowhere
an intregal part of it. Only apparent result of several centuries of
missionary work was as object lessons of better mode of life.

Sia Buffalo Dancer

Performers of dance were two young men with headdresses of buffalo hair and horns and girl with usual female dance costume and small pair of horns. Dance was very strenuous, simulating actions of buffalo and readily understood by watchers.

Kyello—Santo Domingo

Iahla ("Willow")—Taos

The Water Carriers

Fine Baskets of Nevada

Zuni - Tewa

. . . stone house people of the desert

Washing Wheat—San Juan

Threshed with the aid of animals and winnowed by being tossed in the breeze, wheat was placed in loose mesh baskets and submerged in water. Particles of earth were so dissolved, floating bits of straw and chaff scooped off. It was then thoroughly dried in the sun and stored in bags.

Edward Curtis found the Tewa occupying five villages in the Rio Grande valley and one pueblo adjacent to the Hopi villages on East Mesa in Arizona. San Juan, Santa Clara and San Ildefonso were the villages on or near the banks of the river, Nambe and Tesuque in the broken land of t h e valley floor.

The language was Tanoan, which Curtis thought was probably related to the Kiowan, and the northernmost Tewas showed a strong infusion of plains Indian blood, although m o s t outward characteristics were of Spanish and Mexican influence.

Fruit Gatherer—San Ildefonso

"Among the valued gifts of the early Spanish priests was the peach," Curtis explains. "In every pueblo orchard are scrubby, twisted peach trees which without cultivation, yield small fruit of good flavor. This girl is Povi-Tamu (Flower Morning). The word 'flower' is a favorite concept in Tewa names, both masculine and feminine."

"The Zuni," Curtis wrote, "lineal descendants of the people of those glamorous Seven Cities of Cibola so eagerly sought by the conquistadores, occupied a portion of the site of Halona, one of those all b u t prehistoric towns on the north bank of the Zuni River in the extreme western part of New Mexico."

Yet he found the people with little historic sense, mainly interested in their small, closely bound world and in its divine institution. "The Zuni believes the earth is flat, joined at the edges to the sky. Below it are four smaller worlds and below those darkness. The visible sun is a bright shield borne by t h e Sun Father. In the East he breakfasts in the house of his sister, then holding up a fox skin, he brings dawn . . . in the West he goes down into the ocean to the house of his grandmother who feeds him before he travels on beneath the earth to his sister's house."

81

A Corner of Zuni

The chamber at left with the ladder poles projecting from the hatchway, is kiva of the north. Many dances were performed for Curtis in this plaza. The dark material piled against the houses is sheep dung for firing pottery.

Oyi—Tsa ("Duck White")
Summer Cacique of Santa Clara

Each Tewa pueblo, Curtis found, was dominated by two native priests, so-called caciques, one in charge of religious activities from the end of February to end of October, the other the rest of the year. In the biographical section an incident is included to illustrate the power these caciques held over the civil authorities.

The Offering—San Ildefonso

A pinch of corn tossed into the air as an offering to various deities, especially the sun, was a formality to begin the Tewa day.

Offering at the Waterfall—Nambe

Feather offerings are deposited in numerous shrines, buried in the earth near pueblos and placed in springs, streams and lakes to win the favor of the cloud gods.

Zuni Governor

"The form of Zuni civil government was imposed upon them by the Spaniards," Curtis noted. "Governor and assistant are appointed annually by a group of six so-called rain priests, associated with world regions; two war chiefs and Chief Old Woman. But the real power in the community is invested in four hierarchical groups. Most important individual is the North Chief."

Chaiwa—Tewa

Southern Cheyenne - Arapaho
Comanche - Oto - Wichita - Quapaw

. . . in the wooded hills of Oklahoma

On the Canadian River

The Comanche were not native to Oklahoma but placed t h e r e in Curtis' time for riddance. Their central habitat had been the headwaters of the Platte River, assumed to be the same as that of the Shoshone. Attracted by the great herds of wild horses southward, which had been i n t r o d u c e d by the Spaniards, they moved south. The buffalo gave them ample food and with plenty of horses they could range far afield. Their most frequent raids were on the Pecos and other villages of the peaceful Pueblos of New Mexico, whom they regarded as Mexicans. This hostility affected the white pioneers of Texas from which state they were finally driven.

The Cheyenne and Arapaho were of Algonquian origin, making a great migratory march to the Great Plains in former times. Tribal differences over the 1825 treaty with t h e government caused one faction to go south. "Story of the strife between the Cheyennes and whites," said Edward Curtis, "is tragic to both sides and one of the darkest pages in our dealings with the Indians."

The Oto were still growing substantial crops in the Southwest when noted by the first white explorers but became a hunting tribe with the abundance of buffalo. They lived in earth lodges similar to those of the early Mandan and Arikara.

85

Comanche Mother and Child

Black Man—Arapaho

John Quapaw (Hunta Wakunta)

The Quapaw were of Siouian stock, originally part of the big tribe on the Mississippi River comprised of Omaha, Ponca, Kansa and Osage. When they moved to the west bank of the Mississippi, north of the Arkansas, they took the Quapaw name, meaning "downstream people."

Cheyenne Chief

Wichita Grass House

The Wichita, affiliated linguistically with Cado, Waco, Tawakoni, Ioni and Pawnee, were referred to as "the grass house people." A sedentary, agricultural tribe, the Wichita offered a strong contrast in physique and culture to the Comanche and other neighbors. In the fall they hunted buffalo and other game.

Lefthand—Comanche

There were no more vigorous people among the plains Indians than the Comanches, as the face of this old brave would indicate. Noted warriors and raiders, they were the enemies of many tribes and extended their depradations even into Mexico.

Standing Two—Oto

Central Prairie Tribes

Teton Sioux - Yanktonai - Assiniboin

. . . on the northern prairies

Camp on the Little Big Horn

Edward Curtis spent many days going over the Custer battlefield on the Little Big Horn foot by foot, from where the U. S. troops left the Rosebud to the ridge where they made the last stubborn fight. "Among the dozens of Indians I questioned," he reported, "was Curley, so often called the sole survivor of the Custer fight. He has been so bullied, badgered, questioned . . . and called a liar . . . that I doubt if today, if his life depended on it, he could tell if he was ever at or near the fight.

"I was particularly interested in getting the Indian point of view as to the bravery and respective fighting qualities of the different tribes. The Crows claim the Flatheads were the most worthy foes . . . on the other hand the Blackfoot was brave to recklessness but was foolhardy and lacking in judgment, did not even know when to run. The Sioux were a worthy foe and so greatly outnumbered the Crows that the latter could succeed only by quick, bold strokes, then back into their own country. Many a Crow war party went out to the land of the Sioux never to return."

90

Sioux Girl

High Hawk—Brule

The Teton Sioux or Lakota in early historic times occupied the territory around Big Stone Lake, Minn. They moved gradually westward, driving the Omaha to the south, themselves staying in the valleys of the Big Sioux and James Rivers in South Dakota. Another move took t h e m westward to t h e Missouri River, forcing the Arikara south. They then settled in the Black Hills, sending occasional war parties against the Blackfeet in Central Montana. Tribes related to the Teton Sioux were the Ogalalla, Brule, Miniconjou, Two Kettle, Sans Arc and Hunkpapa.

The Yanktonai constituted the middle division of the Dakotas which made their home along the Missouri River. Their migration was from Mille Lac in eastern Minnesota to the Missouri at the mouth of the White River in South Dakota. In this move they all but exterminated one Mandan village near Bismarck, North Dakota and later raided other Mandan settlements as well as those of the Hidatsa, Arikara, Cree and Assiniboin. Their expeditions extended also to the Northwest, warring with the Blackfeet, Atsina—or Gros Ventres—Apsaroke, Cheyenne and even the Nez Perce in eastern Washington.

Invocation   *Prayer to the Great Mystery*

PRAYER TO THE GREAT MYSTERY

Great Mystery, you existed from the first. The sky, this earth you cre-
   ated; Great Mystery—look upon me, pity me, that the Nation
   may live.
Earth, Father of all, I make this offering; pity me. Chief of all, I make
   this offering; pity me.
Spirit Creatures of the four w i n d s—to you I offer this pipe that the
   Nation may live.
North—this day no other creature may be mentioned; before the face of
   the North, let the Nation live.
Sunrise—no other creature may be mentioned. May there be no adver-
   sity that the Nation may live.
West, Nation of Thunderers—give me a good day that the Nation may
   live.
G r e a t Mystery—you are mighty. Pity me that the Nation may live;
   Great Mystery—help me with an omen, that the Nation may live.

Slow Bull Taking Oath—Ogalalla Sioux

93

Sioux Camp

Jack Red Cloud—Sioux

Slow Bull—Ogalalla

Slow Bull, about 64 when Curtis knew him, was a warrior from the age of 14 when he fought against the Apsaroke with Red Cloud's party. In his lifetime he had 55 battles with the Apsaroke, Shoshoni, Ute, Pawnee, Blackfoot and Kutenai. On one occasion when charging Apsaroke, his horse stepped in a hole and fell, the enemy warrior leaping on him. Slow Bull struck out with his bow, leaped on another horse as a second Apsaroke attacked. Slow Bull dispatched him with a hatchet and killed the first attacker.

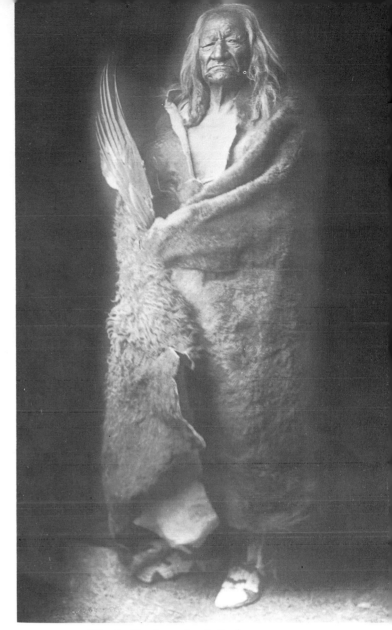

Black Eagle—Assiniboin

Under no circumstances would Chief Black Eagle talk to Curtis to the point of giving him information. No amount of persuasion or argument would bring him to friendliness. So stubborn was he, Curtis expected trouble when Black Eagle came to his tent at three o'clock in the morning. In the eerie blackness he said he had now learned Curtis was writing a book and that he would be in it. "You will if you tell me something to put in it," Curtis replied. He learned Black Eagle had been talking to other braves and was a changed man, eagerly recounting his exploits.

The Assiniboin tribe was the result of a split in the Dakotas. About 1600 people deserted that tribe in anger over a wrong done a chief's wife, moved north and east to Rainy Lake and Lake Nipigon, north of Lake Superior. They were friends of the Cree, lifetime enemies of the Dakota.

Crazy Thunder—Ogalalla   *Hollow Horn Bear—Brule*

TETON SIOUX BUFFALO CHASE

With the Teton S i o u x and most of the prairie tribes the buffalo hunt was n e v e r considered lightly as a game or some high-spirited recreation. Winter or summer, it was a serious tribal function attended by much ceremony, as became the devout nature of the people. The buffalo stood between them and starvation and it was hunted with all religious fervor. No individual was allowed to participate unless he had made proper obeisance to the spirits.

After p r a y e r s and many songs, scouts were sent to look for the buffalo, the supplications of the others continuing. A watch was kept after the first day for signals from the scouts that game had been sighted. The priests were told and preparations began. A hunting leader was chosen from among the chiefs and special detachments selected and placed under separate leaders. They proceeded to t h e place where the herd was grazing and made a wild sweep on the stupid but fleetfooted animals.

In earlier times when buffalo were plentiful the hunters made a circular camp around t h e m, tipis pitched close together to prevent any escape. Two young men with waka bows and arrows ran around the trapped animals, singing medicine songs to bring them under a spell so the hunters could close in for the slaughter. By later methods, many of which Edward Curtis witnessed, the kill was made by driving them into a compound or stockade of logs and brush set at the foot of some abrupt depression if possible.

In mountainous r e g i o n s the buffalo were driven over cliffs to be crushed to death, the solid mass forcing the forward line ahead and over the brink by its own momentum. By another Sioux method a fence or brush line was built, the hunters concealing themselves behind it. When the herd was driven between the lines, the men rose up shouting and waving their arms, stampeding the quarry toward a sharp gully, swamp or snowbank. Sometimes one hunter would don a buffalo robe and run before the confused herd by way of supplying a leader. The buffalo appeared to have no sense of self-preservation.

Planning a Raid

Apsaroke - Hidatsa

. . . in the pine forests, mountains and prairies of Montana

Chief and his Aides

The Apsaroke were a Siouian tribe familiarly known as Crow. Edward Curtis appraised them as the most highly developed primitive American hunters and warriors. "They clothed themselves better, dwelt in finer lodges, decked their horses in trappings so gorgeous as to arouse the wonder of early explorers. They excelled all other tribes in the Rocky Mountain region—were brave, devoted to supernatural forces that gave them strength against enemies. Their social laws prevented intermarriage, hardships of life eliminated weaklings, and the women—as strong as men—did not bring forth puny offspring. The Crow repelled constant invasions of Sioux, Cheyenne, Arapaho to the e a s t, Flathead and Nez Perce to the west, Blackfoot to the north.

98

Winter Camp—Hidatsa

Also a Siouian tribe but vastly different from the Crow w e r e the Hidatsa, inaccurately known as the "Gros Ventres of the Missouri." They were a sedentary people of semi-agricultural nature, their habitat along the Missouri River from the Heart River to the Little Missouri in North Dakota. Their history records a separation from the Apsaroke because they lacked the will and strength to carry on extensive predatory warfare.

99

Upshaw

Upshaw was of inestimable value to Edward Curtis as interpreter and scout, for example in the search for the Sacred Turtles in the Mandan country. (Vol. IV *North American Indian*.) He was educated, the son of Crazy Pend d'Oreille.

Shot In The Hand—Apsaroke

Shot In The Hand was a Mountain Crow obtaining hawk medicine by fasting. In this rite he had a powder of hawk's heart, mixed with sweet grass and green paint, eating some before going into battle. He lacked medicine to become big war leader, was shot attacking Piegans but rose and charged, was again shot and rolled down hill. He claimed he struck seven times under fire, was challenged by Ogalalla Chief Red Cloud who boasted of same four times. When father was killed he retrieved body, was shot in arm. He "threw away" seven of eight wives.

Hoop On The Forehead—Apsaroke

A Mountain Crow, the son of Bull Chief, Hoop On The Forehead first fasted at 18. When he offered finger to the sun, he received a vision which brought a pistol in battle. Fasted three times more, each time self-inflicting bodily torture, each time receiving vision. Took part in 33 war expeditions, was never leader but scout with Generals Crook, Miles, Howard and Gibbon.

A Mountain Fastness

Two Leggings—Apsaroke

Two Leggings, a River Crow, was adopted into the Tobacco order by Bull Goes Hunting, who gave him medicine of fossil roughly shaped like horse facing both ways, and he became war leader. In pursuing Piegans who had killed a woman in an Apsaroke camp across the Big Horn River from Fort C. F. Simth, he counted dakshe and captured gun. Later he led two parties against Hunkpapa Sioux and took several scalps. He also seized 50 horses from Yanktonai at Fort Peck and with Deaf Bull led a party which brought back 80 horses from Teton Sioux.

Wolf—Apsaroke

Born in 1857, Wolf obtained Wolf medicine by purchase. He possessed dakshe and captured gun, both honors won when he rushed into a hollow where two Yanktonai, who had killed and wounded several Apsaroke, were concealed. In another battle, when six of a party of seven turned back without finding enemy, Wolf found the camp and captured a tethered horse stolen by Yanktonai. He pursued them, was wounded when horse fell.

Medicine Man—Hidatsa

Watching for the Signal

Scouts have halted on hilltop to reconnoitre position of enemy. Meanwhile the main war party, miles to the rear, watches the scouts. If they start running in zig-zag fashion, the chiefs know enemy has been sighted and gather their forces for the charge.

Red Wing—Apsaroke

Red Wing was a Mountain Crow of the Peigan Lodge clan, Lumpwood society. He obtained no medicine by fasting but purchased that of brown crane and owl, led a successful war party with it. Captured two guns in battle. Was U. S. scout at Fort Custer, accompanied a detachment of troops in pursuit of Sioux horse raiders. The latter surrendered and Red Wing claimed dakshe since he had been the first to touch the enemy. (The honor dakshe was given for striking an enemy first. If enemy was living and active, an eagle feather was fastened upright in back of hair. It dead, the feather drooped.)

Apsaroke Medicine Tipi

Mandan - Arikara - Atsina

...in the Missouri River region of North Dakota

Spotted Bull—Mandan

White Shield—Arikara

The Mandan, Arikara and Atsina were neighbors but linguistically different. The Mandan, in western North Dakota, were not warrior people, willing to defend by fighting but not predatory. Edward Curtis heard their chiefs boast of war prowess and saw a fair collection of scalps but judged them far short of the Sioux and even the Hidatsa. Corn was their main staple but they depended on buffalo meat. In six populous Mandan villages, with thousands of warriors, he found almost no full b l o o d s. They were hardly a shadow of their former greatness mainly due to the ravages of d i s e a s e in an earlier period, 1738 to 1804.

The Arikara tribe was an offshoot of the Pawnee, familiarly known as Arikaree, their villages in Curtis' visits being at intervals along the Missouri River at the mouth of the Platte. They were tribal enemies of the Mandan and Hidatsa but were sometimes at peace with them. During an earlier migration they had been beset by the Wichita, Comanche, Kiowa, Cheyenne, Apsaroke and Sioux. It had been said they could not claim any friends—all whites and Indians were hostile. They became the pawns of fur traders and rival U. S. politicians.

Of Algonquian stock, the Atsina were a branch of the Arapaho, their historical habitat in the foothills of the Rockies in northern Montana, prior to the arrival of the Blackfoot. The Atsina repelled S i o u x attacks, made alliance with Blackfoot. Curtis found them one of the most agreeable and tractable tribes he encountered. They were buffalo hunters, raising no crops.

105

Arikara Medicine Ceremony—Dance
of the Black Tailed Deer

Bull Neck—Arikara

At 16 Bull Neck and six other Arikara floated down the Missouri River and ran horses out of a Sioux encampment. On another raid in a party of twenty-five Arikara, he found a stray horse belonging to white wood cutters who told him of some Sioux nearby. Party attacked one Sioux and two Arikara killed. He participated in many other raids on Sioux, some in retaliation for attacks on his village.

Arikara Medicine Ceremony—The Ducks

Three members of the order are painted to represent ducks, holding rushes from the nest, as they dance around the sacred cedar.

Arikara Medicine Fraternity—The Prayer

Assiniboin Boy—Atsina

This youth went on the warpath at 18, was married at 22. He counted coups in a fight against the Peigan when 21 of them were killed. He slew one with a Piegan knife. In another battle he killed two Piegan horses and shot a man in both legs.

Bear's Belly—Arikara

Bear's Belly was born in 1847. He joined General Custer's scouts at the age of 19. On encountering five tipis of Sioux, Bear's Belly counted two first coups and one second. He fasted but once—an old man giving him advice together with buffalo skull and commanding him to smear his body with white clay. The old man cut several strips of flesh from Bear's Belly's breast and gave them to the skull. He was married at 19, was a member of the Bears in the medicine fraternity.

Arikara Medicine Ceremony—Dance
of the Fraternity

Arikara Girl

Alsina Woman

Mandan Fisherman

Badland and Mountain Tribes

Piegan - Northern Cheyenne

. . . in the badlands and mountains of the northern prairies

At the Water's Edge—Piegan

In a Piegan Lodge

Edward Curtis identified Little Plume and his son, Yellow Kidney, occupying position of honor (in the photograph above) at rear of lodge opposite entrance. "Note the ever-present pipe and accessories on tobacco cutting board. From lodge poles hang buffalo skin shield, long medicine bundle, eagle-wing fan, deerskin articles for dressing horse. Upper end of rope is attached to juncture of lodge poles and in stormy weather lower end is made fast to stake in center of floor space."

After the Teton Sioux had pushed the Cheyenne out of the Black Hills, they moved westward and northward to the headwaters of the Powder River and foothills of the Big Horn Mountains where they conflicted with the Apsaroke. They then went south to the heads of the North Platte River from which the Kiowa had fled. On November 27, 1867, Gen. Custer dealt the Cheyenne a crushing blow at the Battle of Washita. This gave Custer a great reputation as an Indian fighter and Edward Curtis conjectured: "The ease with which he won the fight probably caused him to underestimate the fighting ability of the Sioux when he met them on the Little Big Horn in 1876."

Sun Dance Encampment

Tribal assembly for Sun Dance, 1898—230 tents of Blackfoot and Bloods from Canada—on Piegan reservation in northern Montana near Browning.

PIEGAN SUN DANCE

The Sun Dance of the Piegans, said Edward Curtis, was one of the most profound displays he ever saw in his entire Indian experience. "It is wild, terrifying and elaborately mystifying. The first time I witnessed it I sat in the hallowed lodge with my friend George Bird Grinnell, who was called the 'Father of the Blackfoot people.' It was at the start of my concerted effort to learn about the plains and to photograph their lives, and I was intensely affected.

"The Blackfoot Sun Dance is a ritual of self-torture for the ambitious young braves who voluntarily seek fulfillment of the vow to realize the wish of their hearts or to prove their valor. It begins with the purification of the soul. Each brave is confined to a lonely spot miles away from camp until June. Then the call goes out to all neighboring tribes and thousands come to feast, give presents to the p o o r and f o r m alliances with hostile tribes.

"Two days are taken up in forming the great Sun Dance circle, sometimes a mile in diameter. The placing of tribes and dignitaries, the herding of the common people, all this is arranged by masters of ceremony and criers carrying tufted, beaded wands. On the third day warriors are selected to go in search of the mystery tree and this is a very colorful panoply. In feathered war bonnets, mounted on spirited horses, the warriors compete for the honor by recounting their great deeds over and over again, accompanied by the mournful wails of women who have suffered and lost children in enemy raids.

"The honored warriors set out on the fourth day, bringing back the message that one of them has found the mystery tree. The tribal circle is formed in t h e 'mellowed earth space' which the Blackfoot believes represents the unappropriated life power of the earth. Certain trailing sweet grass and sacred wild sage is planted here, a buffalo skull laid on the spot.

"On the fifth day, the army of braves i n full battle array make their assault on the mystery tree. It is a marvelous spectacle in the tender glow of dawn, the sun a red

114

disc just above the horizon. The warriors rein in their horses ready for the charge. Silhouetted against the sun, the solitary figure of an ancient fighter stands facing the e a s t, his arm raised. As the thousands of tribes people crowd close, t h e hand is dropped and the horses leap out, churning up clouds of dust as their heels are flung high. Releasing pent up shouts of savagery and shrill war whoops, the attackers charge the mystery tree and lash it with all the frenzy and fury of primitive passion.

"If the tree stands the withering assault, it is accepted as the sun pole and felled. Under the leadership of the Sacred Woman, to whom no breath of scandal can be attached, the tree is stripped of any remaining leaves and branches, its base fixed tightly in the earth at the place of the skull within the tribal circle. During the d a y preceding the torture, young braves perform ceremonial dances around the pole as they face the sun.

"Now comes the fatal day for the young man who aspires to greatness before his people. He is brought in from his long purifying confinement and taken to the medicine man. Incisions are made on each breast, the skin loosened between the parallel slits and bone skewers slipped under the strips of skin. Another set of cuts is made at the shoulder blades and another pair of skewers inserted. He is now led to the mystery tree pole as blood streams down from the cuts and placed t o face the sun. Long thongs have been attached to the willowy tip of the pole and the lower ends now fastened to the b r e a s t skewers. From the ones at his back the heavy buffalo skull is suspended.

"The drum beat starts—slow, rhythmical sounds to indicate the inexorable movement of time. Weird chants spring up here and there among the press of spectators until the dancers appear in the circle, when the singing swells to a powerful crescendo. The young brave is moving his legs in time to the music, his body arched back in agonizing pain as the pole is bowed and the skull jerks up and down, the full strain centered on the stretched skin and flesh of breast and back.

"Does the youth endure the torture, the physical p a i n and twisting of his inner pressures, until the sun has crossed over the heavens and sunk below the burning prairie? Or has the skin broken loose or the subject fainted in ignominy? That is the test. It is the supreme bending of fates to the will of man or the domination o f gods. Either a new warrior has been made or a lesser man found wanting. It is a moving spectacle, a never-to-be-forgotten experience."

Piegan Dandy

Cheyenne Girl

White Calf—Piegan

Of White Calf—Unistai-Poka—George Bird Grinnell noted he was a chief for about a generation and when known as Feather, signed a treaty with Gov. Stevens of Washington Territory. He was famous as a warrior, later devoting his life to peace between tribes for the good of his people. He had great breadth of judgment—was kindly, benevolent and gentle. Under threats or bullying, he was unmovable yet quick to acknowledge his errors and modify his views. He foresaw the end of the buffalo, adapted himself and his people to it.

Three Chiefs—Piegan

The Piegan, Bloods and Blackfoot were closely related being allied Algonquian tribes, usually called Blackfeet. They were formerly forest Indians, traditionally of Little Slave Lake country, moving generally east and south, finally settling on the buffalo plains of Alberta and Montana. The tribes were all badly depleted, struck by disease, debauched by f u r traders with liquor and carnal traffic, then suffered a starvation winter, "the result of official stupidity," said Edward Curtis, "coupled with the disappearence of the buffalo. Dr. George Bird Grinnell in his *Blackfoot Lodge Tales* so graphically describes that fearful siege."

The Piegan never were formally at war with the U.S. "But in their intertribal conflicts," Curtis said, "they were very aggressive—a terror to smaller groups. Generally outnumbering their foes they were naturally arrogant and brave in their confidence . . . The Apsaroki said they were the bravest of warriors but lacked the skill to take advantage of their courage. Their aim in warfare was to t a k e scalps and get home. Horses were a most valuable possession of the Piegan and it was a great honor to win them in battle. Those captured were usually the best of the enemy's herds. If men were killed in any raid for horses, it usually meant a revenge raid.

A Piegan war party might consist of two men, usually four or five, occasionally as many as a hundred. In most cases there were few fatalities. When a successful warrior wanted to lead a party, he caught his best horse, held his gun high above his head and rode around the camp singing a war song. It was a signal for all who wanted to follow him to start repairing their weapons a n d moccasins. On the following morning the leader saddled, rode away and assembled the men on a nearby hill. In the leader's absence, his father might decorate his horse and ride about camp singing for his son's success.

117

Porcupine—Cheyenne

Crow Eagle—Piegan

Two Moons—Cheyenne

Two Moons was a war leader of the Cheyenne tribe with a long record of bravery. He was one of the Cheyenne fighters at the Battle of the Little Big Horn when Custer's command was annihilated by a strong force of Sioux and Cheyenne.

Prairie and Forest Tribes

Cree - Sarsi - Assiniboin - Blackfoot

. . . in the lake and muskeg country of Western Canada

Sarsi Camp

An Athapascan tribe, the Sarsi came out of the far North, crossed Saskatchewan and became affiliated with the Bloods, Blackfeet and Piegans, all of Algonquian stock. They became typical plains people, following the new religious practices and learned the art of decoying buffalo into stockades and stampeding them over sharp declevities. Single hunters pursued the buffalo on swift horses, trained to dash alongside the plunging animal, then veer off before the wounded beast could gore them. In stalking deer and antelope the hunter often made a headdress of grass and held a bunch of tall, white sage as cover. The Sarsi shown here was 98 when Edward Curtis photographed him.

Cree Tipis

Known as Woods Cree, Bush Cree, Swampy Cree and Maskegon, the tribe in Curtis' time was scattered over the low country between Hundson Bay a n d Peace River drainage, including the plains of Manitoba, Saskatchewan and Alberta and as far east as Quebec. The stock was Algonquian, the Crees closely related to the Chippewas. The birch bark canoe was their traditional conveyance and they could cover thousands of miles from lake to muskeg to lake with only short portages.

The Assiniboin were separated from the Yanktonai Sioux prior to 1640. The northern branch had further divided into two bands and ranged on both sides of the Bow River from t h e Rocky Mountains eastward out upon the prairies.

Since recorded history the Blackfeet ranged the prairies along the Bow River (earlier along the Saskatchewan and Red Deer Rivers) while their allies, the Bloods and Piegans lived respectively on the Belly and Old Man Rivers.

Assiniboin Hunter

Bear Bull—Blackfoot

Titishu-Ghitl! Uhl ("Deer Running")—Sarsi

Placating Spirit of Slain Eagle—Assiniboin

Feathers were needed by Assiniboin and Cree for ornaments and fetishes. Eagles were snared and caught by hunters concealed in brush-covered pits. Edward Curtis noted the rather elaborate ceremonies conducted over the bodies of the dead birds to ease the wrath of the eagle spirits.

Calling The Moose—Cree

Curtis found the Crees masters of imitating the calls of m a l e and female moose in the fall rutting season when animal seeks mate. He used birch bark trumpet to lure moose within gunshot.

Cree Man

Columbia River
Valley Tribes

Yakima - Kittitas - Nespilim - Spokan
Kalispel - Flathead - Kutenai

. . . in the sagebrush and pine west of the Northern Rockies

Camp on the Yakima

At the time Edward Curtis made his studies there were several small tribes living in the sagebrush lands and along the mountain sources of the Columbia River. They were important only in their combined unity to attempt to maintain independence.

The Yakima represented three small bands on the eastern slopes of the Cascade Mountains in Washington Territory, dwelling in houses built of cottonwood poles, thatched with smaller ones covered with rush matting and earth. They hunted and fished the larger rivers in the spring and fall, dug r o o t s until midsummer, picked berries in the mountains and fished until freezing weather.

The Kittitas were one of the Yakima groups living on the creek by that name flowing into the upper Yakima River. They took a leading part in the 1855 uprising after the treaty was made with Isaac I. Stevens, first governor of Washington Territory. The Nespilim occupied the valley of that stream. Like their neighbors, the Sanpoel, they long refused to hold any communication with representatives of the government although at the time of Curtis' visit, they were within the Colville Reservation.

126

Rush Gatherer in Reed Boat—Flathead Lake

The Kalispel lived in northeast Washington in the valley of the Pend d'Oreille R i v e r from the Idaho line south to Box Canyon. Not addicted to war, they were reckless fighters when aroused, many of their horses obtained by raids on the Coeur d'Alenes, Nez Perce and Yakima. They acquired the custom of scalping from the Flatheads. They made an annual summer trip by canoe and horse to the buffalo plains to hunt through the winter, returning home in the spring with huge loads of meat and skins.

The three Spokan tribes lived below the Coeur d'Alenes along the Spokane River, each holding certain fishing and camping grounds but all sharing the prairies south of the river for root digging and and the hills for berries. They were at war with the U.S. but once, in 1858, when they defied forces from Forts Simcoe and Walla Walla.

The Kutenai were not related by language with any other tribe, occupied the southeastern part of British Columbia between the Rocky Mountains and Kootenay Lake, the valley of the Kootenay River in northern Idaho and extreme northwest corner of Montana. They originally possessed a high type of culture and character but in Curtis' time had degenerated in ragged, filthy, crippled and lazy groups.

The Flatheads controlled the valleys of Clark's Fork of the Columbia River and its tributaries, t h e Bitterroot, Hell's Gate and Flathead—in Montana. They were closely related to the Pend d'Oreille, constantly harassed by war parties of tribes which had less to eat, the Shoshone and Piegan. They lived on deer, elk and fish, made annual trips to the buffalo country of the Missouri which the Piegan, Apsaroke and Atsina tried to control.

By the River—Flathead

Luqaiot—Kittitas

Luqaiot was the son of Ohai, who as chief of the Salishan band in the Kittitas Valley, Washington Territory, at first appeared to favor the Stevens' treaty of 1855, but who was drawn into the uprising by the actions of another son, Qahlchun, in killing some prospectors. At the end of the conflict, Luqaiot made his home among the Spokan, taking as wife a chief's daughter who was the widow of his executed brother, Qahlchun.

Inashah—Yakima

Inashah was an old Yakima of the ruling class which felt the same dislike and suspicion of the white man as their fathers did in the uprising of 1855 when they attempted to expel these newcomers from their territory. Curtis noted in their faces the inherent tribal antipathy, engendered by the white man's greed and aggression.

Flathead Dance

Village of the Kalispel

Dusty Dress—Kalispel

Nespilim Man

Flathead Camp on the Jocko

Embarking on Flathead Lake

On Spokane River

Nez Perce - Walla Walla - Umatilla Wisham - Cayuse - Chinook

. . . in the pine-forested valleys of the Columbia and its tributaries

Cayuse in Holiday Trappings

The Nez Perce tribe populated the watershed of the Clearwater and Salmon Rivers of Idaho, the Palouse in Washington and the Blue Mountain area of Oregon. Intellectually, culturally and physically, they were the leaders of the aborigines of the Columbia River basin and made a marked impression on explorers, traders, missionaries and army officers. They had no tribal organization, were made up of loosely associated bands, yet from the day they were first seen by Lewis and Clark to the close of the Nez Perce War in 1877, all in contact with them said they were an unusual people.

They were primarily eaters of fish, rarely buffalo hunters. Various bands met in May to dig camas roots and for competition in horse racing, gambling and war dances. They spent the next four months fishing on lakes and rivers, then hunted in the mountains.

133

Piopio-Maksmaks—Walla Walla Brave

This man was the son of the Walla Walla of the same name who negotiated the treaty with Gov. Stevens of Washington Territory in Walla Walla Valley, 1855. Father was killed while captive of Oregon volunteers and son then lived with Nez Perce, having married a woman of that tribe. Curtis noted the strong face, piercing eye, indicating courage of family and tribe.

On the Beach—Chinook

The Wisham were a Chinookan tribe with villages scattered along t h e Columbia River. Their houses were of rived planks and timbers. They fished salmon, did not hunt, dug roots and plants from hillsides and meadows, traveling only by canoe. Their life, Curtis found, was of indolent, licentious ease resulting in filth and lack of dignity. Not militant, they bartered for slaves with other Columbia tribes.

Most of these were of Chinookan stock with permanent villages on both sides of the river from The Dalles to the Pacific Ocean—about 175 miles. Life was based on the use of slaves as trade items, an ordinary family having two or three, a wealthy one as many as ten. Polygamy was practiced, a rich man having as many as eight wives all living in the same house.

In 1811 the trading post of Astoria was established and in 1825 the Northwest Company built Fort Vancouver across the Columbia opposite the mouth of the Willamette River. Through this influence and contact with rough, lawless men, a great toll was taken of the Chinooks by smallpox, measles, cholera and whisky. The cholera epidemic of 1830 almost exterminated two populous villages and many drunken parties were drowned when canoes capsized in turbulent Columbia.

Wisham Spearing Salmon in Columbia River

Umatilla Maid

Two distinct cultural areas are represented in this girl's dress—beadworked deerskin of the plains—basketry hat and shell bead necklace of the Pacific Slope. Skin of deer's tail fastened front of collar, was aid in removing garment.

The Walla Walla was a strong group inhabiting the valley of that river at the eastern bank of the Columbia. The Umatilla lived in that river valley in Oregon, a tribe with speech much like the Yakima. The Cayuse, sullen, arrogant and warlike, ranged near the Blue Mountains to the John Day River in Oregon. Part of this tribe, scientists conjecture, may have split off and become the Molalla between the Cascade Mountains and Willamette River. Cayuse slaughtered whites at Marcus Whitman Mission.

Nez Perce Babe

Nez Perce War Chief

Chief Joseph

Nez Perce Chief Joseph's name was better known than any Northwest Indian's. In popular opinion he is given credit for the remarkable Nez Perce flight from Idaho to Northern Montana in the War of 1877. The unfortunate Nez Perce effort to retain what was rightfully their own is unparalleled in the annals of Indian resistance to greed of whites, so few tribes rising in the last struggle against dishonest and relentless subjection.

Chinooks Setting Out to Sea from Lower Columbia

The Columbia reaches the Pacific Ocean in a broad estuary between low, flat shores, then bold and wooded. The conflict of winds, tide and currents raises treacherous seas and made skilled canoemen of the Chinooks.

Southwest Coast Tribes

Hupa - Klamath

. . . in the Trinity River region of northern California

Fishing from Canoe—Hupa

The Hupa, Yurok and Karok were the principal tribes in the Trinity River area of northern California, and they even more than other peaceable Indians, suffered greatly at the hands of the whites by force and false pretenses. They lived in small, isolated groups, lacked the social instinct and strength for self-defense against any strong force. Edward Curtis found the Hupa high in material culture with marked similarities to the tribes north along the Pacific Coast, with stress laid on the acquisition of wealth as the necessary basis of rank. Woodworking was important, salmon a staple food with acorns, slavery in a modified form an institution and ceremonial life highly developed.

Hupa Woman

In the Forest—Klamath

Except in cold weather, the upper part of the Hupa woman's body
was bare. Hanging from girdle about the waist was a knee-length
fringe apron made of pine nut shells strung on grass. Deerskin
skirt was open in front to reveal apron. Robes, moccasins, leggings
and basketry hat were sometimes added.

Occupying all of what is now Klamath County, Oregon, the Klamath were the larger of the two Lutuami
tribes, the other being the Modoc to the South. Both had their share of trouble with immigrants and
soldiers, suffering accordingly. Prior to a treaty of 1864 they sent slaving expeditions into the Pit River
country, some captives being exchanged for horses. Later they traded deerskins with Yreka settlers, the
trading parties often raided by the local Shasta Indians.

Friendly with the Hupa, the Yurok lived on the banks of the Klamath River as it flowed into the Pacific,
in redwood forests thick with giant bracken, fallen trees and tangled shrubs. From this jungle came
materials for basketry, bows, canoes, houses—from fish in ocean and stream came their main food.

Klamath in War Dress

This entire costume, Curtis noted, was alien to the primitive Klamath. The feathered headdress, fringed shirt, deerskin leggings were adopted during the historical period with other customs and habits of plains culture which extended to Klamath country by way of Columbia River and plains of Central Oregon.

Klamath Warrior's Headdress

Fishing Platform on Trinity River—Hupa

Salmon Stream

Youth is waiting for shadowy outline of young fish lurking in quiet pool as it gathered strength for dash through tiny cascade. Salmon were also taken by hooks and in nets—the barbed hook for trolling from canoe or shore and for set line stretched between stakes and left overnight.

Hupa Jumping Dance Costume

The Hupa Jumping Dance was an annual ceremony for averting pestilence—the headdress a wide band of deerskin with red woodpecker crests, narrow edging of white deer hair. Deerskin robe was worn as kilt, each performer displaying all the shells and beads he possessed or could borrow. In the hight hand was carried a straw-stuffed cylinder with slit-like opening from end to end—the significance unknown to the modern Hupa, Edward Curtis said.

144

Pomo - Yokuts - Miwok - Wappo

. . . from the western slopes of the Sierra Nevadas to the redwood rivers of the Coast

Fishing Camp—Lake Pomo

Curtis reported 30 Pomo villages, or rancherias, with populations of f r o m one family to a hundred persons. Seven were in the valley of the Russian River, centering about Ukiah, three in the region of Clear Lake, one on the coast near the mouth of Garcia River and one on headwaters of Middle Fork of Gualala River. Pomo women were highly skilled in basketry, both coiled and twined type. The former were used for containing valued trinkets or paraphernalia of shamans and were ornamented with feathers of redheaded woodpecker or green ones from heads of male mallard ducks. Twined baskets were used for gathering, preparation and serving of food. Pomo men also wove rough baskets for fish and game traps and for carrying wood.

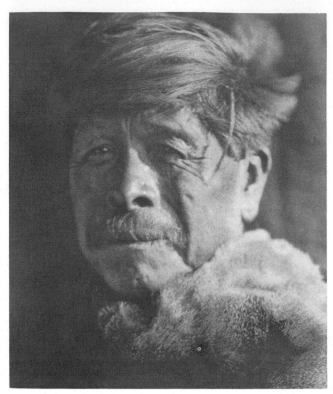

Shatila—Pomo   *Chukchansi Yokut*

The Wappo was a detached Yukian tribe in the Alexander Valley of the Russian River near Healdsburg. Houses were scattered over a wide area in the village which had its own chief and sub-chief. The former sat in state in his house, did not hunt or perform labor of any k i n d, yet was expected to have constant thought about the welfare of his people, plan for their protection and amusement.

The sweathouse was a Pomo tradition, used primarily by men. It was almost subterranean, about eight feet in diameter, excavated two or three feet, roofed by rafters radiating from a heavy post and thatched with brush and long grass. Heat for sweating was provided by fire inside, most of smoke finding its way out doorway. After remaining inside as long as possible, perhaps half an hour, men would come out and plunge themselves into lake or stream.

Generally the area of the Yokuts was the entire vast plain of the San Joaquin Valley. They knew little about warfare, made small raids to steal women and other booty without fighting. They used a few crude implements of bone and stone, made bows of laurel or oak saplings with strings of sinew or milkweed cord. Reed arrows were carried in skin quivers. Their tobacco pipes were of manzanita wood, their greatest handiwork basketry.

The Fisherman—Southern Miwok

146

A Wappo   *Pomo Girl*

The principal Miwok area lay on the western slope of the Sierra Nevada to the San Joaquin valley and between the Fresno and Consumnes Rivers the region including California's Yosemite and giant Sequoias. Living in the high country in the summer, they fled the heavy snows and spent autumn and winter in the foothills to harvest acorns, grass seeds, t u b e r s and bulbs, to kill game a n d fish the teeming streams.

Pomo clothing was of the simplest kind. Men ordinarily were completely naked, women wearing short kilts of shredded tules hanging in a thick mass of fringe about the thighs. In cold weather both sexes wore rabbit skin robes and when rainy, armless, knee-length capes of shredded tules. Hats were unknown and feet always bare.

Diegueno - Paviotso - Cahuilla - Mono

. . . from the southern Sierra deserts to the Pacific

Mono Home

Edward Curtis placed the habitat of the Mono in east-central California including all of Mono County and Inyo County as far south as Owens Lake. On the west were the towering peaks of the Sierra Nevada, in the basin a series of valleys northward to the Nevada line—Big Pine, Independence, Lone Pine, Bishop, Round Valley, Long Valley, Mono Lake and headwaters of Walker River.

The wickiup shown above is a typical winter shelter with burden b a s k e t s and sieves of winnowing trays. House was 12' to 14' in diameter. A shallow pit was dug, green willow poles set close together around it, bent over and bound at top. Battens were lashed around outside and many courses of dry grass applied, then green grass or cattail leaves. Doorway was on east side, hole left at peak for smoke.

The Cahuilla lived generally in the area of California's Salton sink, the San Jacinto Mountains and headwaters of San Luis Rey and Santa Margarita rivers. "They wore little clothing," Curtis noted, "perhaps a skin loincloth for men and short kilt of mesquite bark fringe for women, s u p p l e m e n t e d on occasion by robes made of strips of rabbit fur."

Desert Cahuilla Woman

The Primitive Artist—Paviotso

The Paviotso were in the northeast corner of California and north-western Nevada. They were more alert and active, less sullen than many southern California tribes. Avaricious and predatory, they resented intrusions into their territory. They had difficulties with the Mono, are thought to have killed, among other trappers and explorers, Peter Lassen, for whom mountain is named.

Southern Diegueno

Territory of the Diegueno Indians coincided with what is now San Diego County. Curtis found it an elevated region breaking into lofty, rounded hills with many canyons. The villages or rancherias in the uplands were not occupied in summer, the Dieguenos roaming in search of edible foods culminating in the acorn harvest.

Before the White Man—Palm Canyon

Palm Canyon at the eastern base of the San Jacinto Mountains on Agua Caliente reservation, was occupied by Cahuilla Indians—the area now known as Palm Springs.

Hesquiat Root Digger

Northwest Coast Tribes

Suquamish - Skokomish - Snoqualmu
Lummi - Quilcene - Quinault

. . . on the forested rivers and sounds of western Washington to the sea

Tsasalatsa—Skokomish

Snoqualmu Type

The Salishan tribes east and west of the Cascade Mountains constituted one of the most widespread and numerous family groups of North American Indians. The Coast Salish, represented by many diverse tribes, speaking dialects of a common language, fished, hunted, gathered roots and berries in the dense forests of fir, spruce and cedar down to the marshy flat lands of Puget Sound. There were many variations in culture and habits between the Cowichan on the north and the Cowlitz on the south, yet Edward Curtis found them possessing many common traits. In stature and mentality they were inferior to the average interior Indians—the body short, legs bowed after generations of squatting in canoes, the heads flattened by binding processes in infancy.

Lummi Type

Primitive Quinault

Living on the shores of the Pacific Ocean, the Quinault were a hardy type of sea hunter and builder of fine canoes. Like all Coast Salish, their women wore nothing but knee-length kilts or thick cedar bark except when cold or rain made goat hair or vegetable fibre blankets or capes more desirable.

Before Curtis' time, the Lummi, with the Samish and Semiahmoo, controlled the islands of northern Puget Sound. There were no streams on these rocky humps for fishing and they gradually pressed to the mainland to net and spear salmon and to dig clams on the sandy shores and delta of the Nooksack River. This aggression resulted in a war with these natives over fishing rights.

The Skokomish were a band of the Twana, living on Hood Canal, which led off the Strait of Juan de Fuca. They never invaded the territory of other tribes but stood their ground valiantly when Snohomish or Chimakum warriors came raiding by canoe or Cowlitz men by foot. They traded with the Clallam to the north, Chehalis to the east and with tribes traveling down t h e Columbia River bringing hemp fibre and mountain goat hair.

Dip-Netting in Pools

Suquamish Girl

The Snoqualmu, as Curtis knew them, were river people living in the villages on the Tolt and Snoqualmie Rivers east of Puget Sound—the Suquamish on Bainbridge Island across the Sound from Seattle.

There was constant internal strife between the Puget Sound tribes which included the Snoqualmu and Suquamish but they united in common defense on many occasions when the strong tribes from the north, Kwakiutl and Cowichan particularly, came sweeping down in their big canoes to capture women and children for slaves.

Fishing Camp—Skokomish

Lelehalt—Quilcene

The mustache on this Quilcene does not indicate white ancestry, Curtis concluded. Early travelers noted many men of Pacific Coast tribes who had hair on the face.

Kwakiutl

. . . on Canada's western mainland and Vancouver Island shores

Kotsuis and Hohhuq—Nakoaktok

Two masked performers in winter dance representing mythical birds—servitors in house of man-eating monster, Pahpaqalanohsini. Mandibles were controlled by strings.

In Edward Curtis' findings, the Kwakiutl tribes composed one b r a n c h of the Wakashan linguistic family, occuping generally the western mainland and islands of British Columbia and the eastern shores of Vancouver Island. The name is the Anglicized form of the native Qagyuhl. The tribes came in contact with the Cowichan and Squamish on the south, Bella Coola, Tsimshiam and Haida on the north.

Curtis found the people as mysterious, gloomy and inhospitable as the rainy, foggy, rocky and deeply forested country they lived in. "They seem lost in dark forebodings . . . and one is i m p e l l e d to question their knowledge of any such thing as spiritual exhaltation or mental pleasure except such as may be aroused by the gratification of savage passions or purely physical instincts. Chastity, genuine self-sacrificing friendship, even the inviolability of a guest—a cardinal principle a m o n g most Indian tribes—are unknown. It is scarcely exaggeration to say that no single, noble trait redeems the Kwakiutl character."

The Kwakiutl society consisted of nobility, common people and alien slaves. The noble class was all-powerful, descent reckoned in paternal line. The subservience of lower class was rather that of servant than subject. The Kwakiutl were head hunters but war was the profession of comparatively few men, the greater number on an expedition being canoe paddlers and plunderers. Twenty canoes with average crew of fifteen composed an ordinary war party.

Hamasta in Tluwulahu Costume—Kwakiutl

Principal chief in Kwakiutl ceremony, hamasta is shown in "button blanket," cedar bark neck rings and head band. Right hand grasps shaman's rattle, left the carved staff used as emblem of office. Button designs represent "coppers," symbol of wealth.

Koskimo House Post

Curtis said these interior supporting columns were the most striking carvings of Kwakiutl houses. Figures perpetuate memories of incidents in legendary history of family, often representing tutelary spirit of founder.

Actual coppers were keystone-shaped sheets of copper, upper portion hammered slightly convex, raised T occupying lower half. The convex surface was coated with graphite w h i c h allowed engraving of some fabulous creature. The price of a copper was not based on its intrinsic value but on the number of times it was sold, price rising with each sale, interest up to 100 per c e n t. Curtis recorded the note that probably the greatest price ever paid for a copper was 20,000 blankets—in the form of blankets, canoes, sailing craft and cheaper coppers—by a Mamalelekala chief in 1909.

Approach of Wedding Canoes

Nakoaktok Chief's Daughter

When Kwakuitl chief held potlach—
ceremonial distribution of property to
all the people—his oldest daughter was
enthroned in this manner, symbolically
supported on heads of her slaves.

Siwit—Awaitala

The Awaitlala were a Kwakiutl tribe possessing rights to fish
for oulachan on Knight Inlet waters. This was a smelt-like fish
with high oil content. When extracted, oil was used with other
foods and extensively for trading with tribes farther south.

On the Beach—Nakoaktok

High-born clam digger wearing aboriginal costume cedar bark blanket and rain cape, spruce root "chief's hat" and woolen ankle bands. Sharpened yew stick was used for digging.

Quahila—Koprino

Young chief of almost extinct tribe on Quatsino Sound, n e a r northwest end of Vancouver Island, wearing nose ornament of dentalium shell, obtained in vast quantities in local waters, used as basis of trade with Northwest Coast tribes.

In physique and intelligence, Curtis found the Quatsino inferior to other Kwakiutl tribes. Note artificial deformation of head, a former custom quite general on Northwest Coast.

Yakotlus—Kwakiutl of Quatsino Sound

Bridal Group

Bride stands in middle between two dancers hired for occasion. Her father is at left, bridegroom's father at right behind man who presides over box drum.

Nootka

Ready to Run the Seas

The Nootka Indians developed canoe building and whaling to a great skill. The men were daring sea hunters, helped by the belief they possessed supernatural powers. A feat so remarkable as the killing of a whale by primitive means was inexplicable to these Indians except on the basis of spiritual assistance. "The most successful whalers," Curtis wrote, "were t h o s e who, even inheriting the profession, found an object representing the supernatural whale—either a double-headed black worm, eleven inches long by an inch and a half thick, or a certain species of crab. If it be the worm he takes it up and preserves it as a charm; if the crab he removes the right claw and breast of the shell."

The Bowman

The Nootka were the second branch of Wakashan stock, the Kwakiutl being the first. They inhabited the western shores of Vancouver Island and the extreme northwestern tip of the U.S., the Cape Flattery area. It was the Nootkas which were first encountered by early explorers Juan Perez, Captain James Cook and the English trader John Mears.

The Clayoquot were one of the better known and more populous Nootka tribes, living on one of the major sounds of the Pacific Ocean. Some of their beliefs varied from those of their neighbors, such as life in an afterworld, and they practiced tattooing extensively. A ring was tattooed around the ankles of female children by stitching a fish line through the skin and drawing after it a nettle fibre blackened with elderberry wood charcoal.

Nootka Women at Clayoquot Sound

Nootka women commonly wore the cedar bark capes over their heads to protect forehead from tump line when carrying burden baskets. The proper use of cape was to shed rain.

Hesquiat Girl

Nootka Whaler Ready for Hunt

Clayoquot Girl

This girl wears a cedar bark ornament tied to the hair of virgins on the fifth morning of puberty ceremony. Curtis said the fact that the girl posing for this picture was the prospective mother of an illegitimate child caused considerable amusement to the onlookers and herself.

Nootka Man

It was commonly believed the facial hair of many Northwest Coast Indians was evidence of intermingled Causcasian blood. Not so, said Curtis. In 1778 Capt. Cook observed—"Many old men have not only considerable beards but whiskers or mustachios."

Nunivak - Kotzebue - King Island
Cape Prince of Wales

. . . on Alaska's tundra and rocky islands

Ready for the Sealing—Nunivak

The kaiak is the most important craft of many Eskimos as their livelihood depends upon it. Men use it to transport themselves from one hunting camp to another and for fishing, spearing waterfowl, pursuing seal and walrus.

Edward Curtis estimated the total Eskimo population of Alaska at the time of his limited investigation, was 12,405. He found the culture of the tribes he visited broadly similar, varying with the distribution and migration of mammals, birds and fish. The Nunivak and King Island people had a pronounced seal culture because they lived directly in the path of the seal and walrus migrations. Whaling was the chief occupation of Cape Prince of Wales Eskimos whose living habits differed from t h e inhabitants of the Kotzebue area who hunted beluga and seal on the water, caribou along the streams.

169

Boys in Kaiak—Nunivak

Eskimo boys were trained in the manly pursuits from their earliest years, honored with feasts on taking their first game.

Since the major part of their food supply came from the sea, Nunivak islanders erected their homes close to the shore facing the water, yet they moved with all belongings to take full advantage of the s e a l run, fish runs, bird and berry seasons. The people at Cape Etolin used five villages and camps throughout the year. Their winter villages, typical of all the permanent settlements, included eight structures—all within an area of fifty by forty-seven paces. A tunnel passed along in front of each row of houses and each set of men's and women's houses were joined by an intersecting tunnel.

Jackson—Interpreter at Kotzebue

With Kotzebue in the center of all Alaska Eskimo activity, the people had brisk trade with natives of other areas who brought furs, tobacco, reindeer skins and stayed to feast and dance.

Cape Prince of Wales Man

Curtis said none but a hardy and fearless people could wrest food, clothing, shelter from such a cruel evironment—a land of unbroken Arctic winds and grinding ice packs. Depleted by disease, Cape Prince of Wales natives had only one village—Kingegan—made up of two settlements.

Kenowun—Nunivak

The nasal septum was pierced, a small ring or hook inserted from which four plain or white beads dangle. For ceremonials or dances, women wear car pendants or rings with flat pieces of ivory and bright colored cloth.

The Noatak winter village was a week's journey by skin boat up the swift, shallow Noatak River from Kotzebue Sound. They hunted and traded with their neighbors, the Kobuk, and the more courageous made a mid-winter journey by dog team to the sea for the early sealing.

Nungoktok—Noatak

Noatak Child

Dahchintok—Nunivak

King Island Homes

Rear parts of houses rest on poles a few feet high or are built against cliff, fronts attached to poles over 20 feet high which project above roofs and with connecting poles serve as drying racks. Houses are usually of two rooms with narrow porch, front room used for storage and second for general living.

INDEX